Micro-teaching

a programme of teaching skills

George Brown : Methuen

To Jessica
and Ben

First published in 1975 by Methuen & Co Ltd
11 New Fetter Lane, London EC4P 4EE
© 1975 George Brown
Printed in Great Britain by
Butler & Tanner Ltd, Frome and London

The cover photograph was taken by Pamla Toler

ISBN 0 416 83010 2 (hardback)
ISBN 0 416 83020 X (paperback)

Distributed in the USA by
HARPER & ROW PUBLISHERS INC.
BARNES & NOBLE IMPORT DIVISION

Contents

Illustrations

Acknowledgements

I should like to thank Professor Alan Milton who as founder director of the Education Centre gave me the opportunity to develop the programme of teaching studies on which this book is based. My thanks are also given to my students, colleagues and friends in the Education Centre and nearby schools for their suggestions and advice ; to Drs Brian McGarvey and John Greer for reading the manuscript ; to Jim Hendry, Denis Joynt and many other UNESCO colleagues working in this field ; and to Professor Ed Stones for his wise counsel. Roy Nash and Routledge are thanked for their permission to quote extracts from *Classrooms Observed,* Professor Ted Wragg and the National Foundation of Education Research for permission to reprint a table and Professor Ned Flanders for permission to reprint his category system. A special word of thanks is given to Sheila McIvor for encouraging me to write this book, and to Morag Stark for her seemingly infinite goodwill and patience in typing it.

A thought for teacher educators:
Why the clever Oxford scholar
lost his supper   *from* A Hundred Merry Tales

A rich franklin in the country, having by his wife but one child and no more, for the great affection that he had to his said child, found him at Oxford to school by the space of two or three years. This young scholar, in a vacation-time for his disport, came home to his father.

It fortuned afterward in a night, the father, the mother, and the said young scholar sitting at supper having before them no more meat but only a couple of chickens, the father said this wise : Son, so it is that I have spent much money upon thee to school, wherefore I have great desire to know what thou hast learned. To whom the son answered, and said : Father, I have studied sophistry, and by that science I can prove that these two chickens in the dish be three chickens. Marry, said the father ; that would I fain see. The scholar took one of the chickens in his hand, and said : Lo, here is one chicken ; and incontinent he took both the chickens in his hand jointly and said, here is two chickens : and one and two maketh three. Ergo here is three chickens. The father took one of the chickens to himself, and gave another to his wife, and said thus : Lo, I will have one of the chickens to my part ; and thy mother shall have another ; and because of thy good argument thou shalt have the third to thy supper, for thou gettest no more meat here at this time – which promise the father kept, and so the scholar went without his supper.

By this tale men may see, that it is great folly to put one to school to learn any subtle science which hath no natural wit.

Section One   On teaching and microteaching

Microteaching: Programme of teaching skills

Some preliminary remarks

This book has been written to help students and young teachers to develop their basic teaching skills. It deals with lesson planning, the perception of teaching and the performance skills of exposition, questioning and discussion. It also contains advice on setting up a microteaching programme. There are three sections: Section One contains a brief discussion of teacher education and training, a social skills model of teaching on which the programme is based and a review of studies in school experience and microteaching. It is included because students and teachers are often keenly interested in the justification for a new approach – particularly if it is one in which they are involved. Section Two outlines the skills in detail, and Section Three suggests ways of organizing and extending the programme.

At the outset it is stressed that microteaching is not a substitute for but a preliminary or supplement to school experience. It is not concerned with the intricacies of teaching specific subjects nor with the problems of working in open plan schools or inner city classrooms. Indeed, I would argue that students should not be asked to tackle such work until they have proven competence in basic teaching skills. Without these skills one can never conquer the twin problems of controlling and motivating learners. In mastering them one gains the freedom and confidence to experiment with new approaches.

A seasoned practitioner can easily forget the painful complexities of learning to teach when faced with forty lively, perhaps reluctant, learners. Teacher educators may offer courses in the sociology of the school or the social psychology of the classroom and yet be blind to the implications of such courses: the enormity of the task of learning to teach in a school. In lectures on teaching methods they may quote the nineteenth-century maxim 'proceed from the known to the unknown, the simple to the complex'. Yet these same principles are conspicuously absent from their own teacher training programme. Often such programmes are based upon a better known nineteenth-century notion: the survival of the fittest.

This notion has also pervaded research in teacher education during this century. The dominant theme has been the search for the good teacher. Its yield has not been high (Getzels and Jackson, 1963; Garner, 1973; Morrison and McIntyre, 1973). Personality and intelligence test scores have been related to teaching practice marks and theory of education examination results. Sophisticated statistical techniques have been applied to the data and the outcome has usually been that teachers who are rated highly manifest a wide range of personality and cognitive characteristics. In short, there is no such thing as a good teaching personality.

In contrast, little attention has been paid to the quality of training programmes for teaching. Biddle's assertion that 'we do not know how to define, prepare for or measure teacher competence' (Biddle, 1964, p. 3) is still true. Teaching, it is said, is an art and, by implication, it cannot be taught. Flying jumbo jets or performing heart transplants are also arts which bring together a wide range of skills. Yet no flying school or medical [5] faculty expects its trainees to perform high level feats without first mastering the basic skills. Teaching also has its repertoire of skills. If these cannot be identified and taught then many teacher educators are guilty of a huge confidence trick. But the root of the problem is not that teaching cannot be taught but rather that it is not taught. Rosenshine in his review of teacher preparation concludes that 'the major question raised by these few studies . . . is not whether teacher preparation is worthwhile but whether the teacher preparation is related to classroom practice' (Rosenshine, 1971, p. 208).

In teacher education there is a temptation to sprinkle aphorisms of teaching in lectures and to rely heavily upon the classroom as the only training ground. A similar approach in flying or medicine would lead to highly publicized disasters.

In contrast this book is based upon a systematic approach to learning to teach. It takes as its starting point that teaching is a complex challenge which may best be tackled by simplifying and controlling the first experiences of teaching. It may be read as a series of hints on teaching or it may be used as a course of instruction in a small group teaching situation or microteaching laboratory. But before embarking upon a description of how to use this book it may be as well to consider teaching, school experience and microteaching.

On teaching and microteaching

Whatever else teaching is, it is a many sided activity. It includes giving information, asking questions, explaining, listening, encouraging and a host of other activities. But a description of these activities does not constitute a description of teaching. For each or all of these activities may be used by others – parents, psychotherapists, politicians or salesmen. What distinguishes teaching from other social activities is its intention: that others learn. In philosophical terms, 'teaching' is a task word like 'hunting' or 'fishing' not an achievement word like 'winning' (Ryle, 1949; Smith, 1969a). It follows from this that a person may teach but his pupils may not learn what he intends them to learn. This is an experience we may all have during our first attempts at teaching. When it occurs we need to analyse why we did not succeed and this, in itself, is sufficient justification for developing a model of teaching and a set of rules to help us to locate our errors.

A model of teaching

There are several teaching models one can choose from (Joyce and Weil, 1972) but many of them are complex descriptions which obscure the salient features. I have there-fore chosen one which is ostensibly simple and robust. It is based upon Argyle's social skill model (Argyle, 1970; Cook, 1970) and it is the basis of the microteaching programme developed at the New University of Ulster. Figures 1 and 2 set out the model and its expanded version.

The teacher's intention that his pupils learn can be put in the form 'T intends that

[6]   **Figure 1.** A simple model for the discussion of teaching

T = Teacher
P = Pupils
X = Material to be learnt (concepts, facts, values, skills)

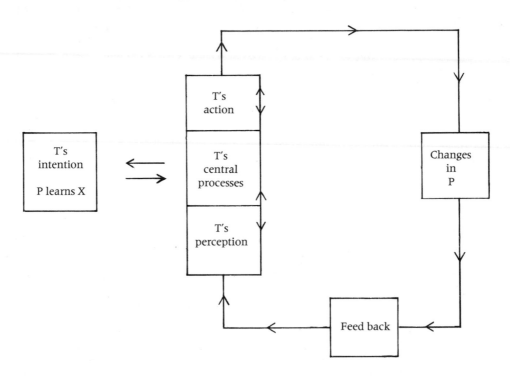

P's learn X', where X may be facts, concepts, values or skills. Interaction between T, P and X may be minimal as, for example, when T lectures upon X to P or it may be intensive, as in a lively discussion between T and Ps about X. The translation of intentions into actions requires the teacher to analyse his task and to choose the most appropriate means of accomplishing his objectives. The teacher has a store of central processes which translate his intentions and plans into actions and performance. This central store contains his linguistic skills, cognitive abilities, personality variables, attitudes and his role expectations of pupils and himself as teacher. These factors shape his repertoire of teaching skills. When these are manifested in actions they produce changes in his pupils. These changes may be immediately signalled to the teacher by the pupils' answers or non-verbal cues. The signals may be intentional or unintentional, simple or complex. Other changes may not be immediately observable and require evaluation and follow-up studies. In this book the term monitoring is used to describe the detection of immediately observable signals and evaluation to describe the detection of long-term changes. The latter is conventionally concerned with cognitive changes. Both monitoring and evaluation are based upon feedback from the pupils' performance. This feedback may or may not be perceived by the teacher – some teachers seem oblivious to signs of boredom. The perception of feedback is determined by the salient central processes of the teacher and his intentions. His intentions may be modified as a result of his perceptions of the pupils and this redirects his central processes to producing other actions. The following simple example from an actual teaching practice may clarify this point.

A student intended to establish a rapport with a class of fourteen-year-olds in a predominantly middle-class school. He began by saying 'Good morning, boys and girls,' expecting them to respond with 'Good morning, sir.' The response he received from one of the pupils was, in fact, 'Piss off, you stupid twit.' He modified his intentions.

You are asked to decide what the student should have done in this situation. Answers which suggest he should not have begun by saying 'Good morning, boys and girls' are not allowable. The problem is one of survival, not of prevention.

This is the first of many teaching problems you will find in the body of the text and in the activities. You are asked to work out your answers before moving to the next sections.

In attempting to answer the above problem you may find many possible strategies each with their own costs and payoffs. As you probe deeper into it you may conclude that one needs to know more about the student teacher and the pupils. This brings us to the expanded version of the model in Figure 2 (*overleaf*).

Just as the teacher may have intentions and a central store of processes so do pupils. In fact they may be learning how to avoid being taught. Their central processes include the norms of group behaviour and their role expectations so admirably described by Hargreaves (1967, 1972); the plethora of personality and cognitive variables beloved by many educational psychologists; the effects of organizational variables and the neglected effects of space, lighting, furniture and fittings (Bennett, 1970). As far as the model and actual teaching are concerned these variables are only important when manifested in behaviour. It is this subtle play of teacher–pupil interactions which is the essence of teaching. For these modify the perceptions, short-term and long-term intentions, the central processes themselves and the behaviour of teachers and pupils.

A model of teacher training

If the business of teaching is complex then learning to teach is even more so. For the student teacher has a twofold intention: that his pupils learn *while* he learns to teach. He has to develop his planning skills, to use and extend his teaching repertoire, to monitor changes in his pupils and to modify his behaviour accordingly. The simplified model of teacher training given in Figure 3 illustrates this point. One can extract from the model three constituents of a teacher training programme – PLANNING, PERFORMANCE and PERCEPTION. Rules for these three Ps of teacher training are acquired by the student in his early experiences of teaching.

In planning lessons a student has to learn to split a topic into its components, specify clearly his objectives and choose the appropriate methods of teaching it. His performance

Figure 2. An expanded model of teaching

T = Teacher
P = Pupils
X = Material to be learnt (concepts, facts, values, skills)

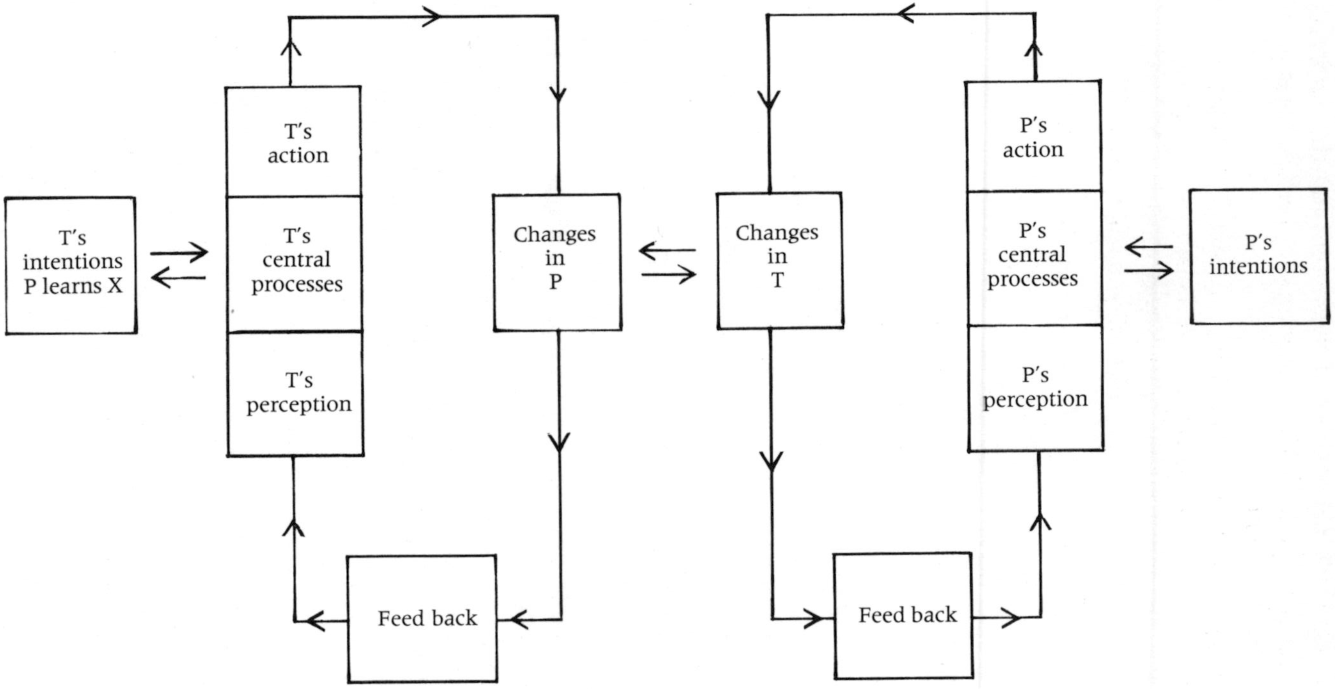

Figure 3. A model for the discussion of teacher training   [9]

ST = Student teacher
P = Pupils
X = Material to be learnt
Y = Skills that ST is intended to learn

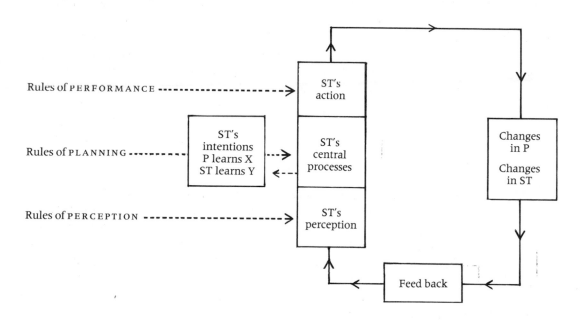

may also be analysed into component skills and these skills consist of patterns of teaching moves and each of these moves is made up of elements of verbal and non-verbal cues. Performance in school experience is only practised at the global level. In microteaching, practice may occur at any level but it is usually focused on the component skills with some global practice as an introduction and as a conclusion to microteaching to bring the skills together into a smooth performance. The perception of teacher-pupil interaction alerts a student to his own teaching behaviours, their effects upon pupils and the changes in the pupils' behaviour. The perceptions may then influence his planning and subsequent performance. But sensitive perceptions of teaching have to be learnt. Merely giving a student the opportunity to observe teaching does not in itself sharpen his perceptions of teaching or improve his technique. He needs to be shown what cues to look for and to be taught which questions to ask himself.

Two linked experiments by the author illustrate this point. An experimental group of students was given feedback based upon teacher-pupil interaction and a control group was given conventional supervision. Both groups were microteaching and they also rated a selected videotaped lesson before and after the microteaching programme of training in order that changes in their perceptions of teaching could be detected. The analyses of results showed that the students in the experimental group had significantly changed their performance but not their perceptions of teaching. In the linked experiment an experimental group of students was given six hours training in the analysis of teacher–pupil interaction and the control group spent six hours observing videotapes without any direction from the experimenter. Both groups were microteaching and they rated the same videotaped lesson before and after the twelve week programme. The analyses of this experiment showed that students in the experimental group significantly changed their perceptions of teaching but the change in their performance was only marginally better than the control group's. Taken together these experiments show that perceptual training sharpened the perceptions of these students, feedback changed their performance (Brown, 1973). Both are, arguably, necessary in a training programme. Training in perception gives a student his own built-in feedback loop which one hopes will continue to persist long after he has completed his preparation for teaching.

Few teacher educators would dispute the importance of acquiring rules of planning, performance and perception. However what a student actually acquires may not be what his lecturers intend him to acquire. Lack of control of the crucial early experiences of teaching may lead to the acquisition of unhelpful teaching habits which may subsequently be difficult to iron out. Discussions between lecturers and students about the key characteristics of planning, performance and perception would certainly help to avoid these problems and improve the training programmes. Such discussions are likely to centre around two foci: the rules which should be acquired and the most effective way of acquiring them. One may conveniently consider these in a discussion of good and successful teaching, school experience and microteaching.

Good teaching

Good teaching is a direct function of the judges' value systems. And judges do not always agree. Barr (1961) in his review of studies of teacher effectiveness had this to say: 'Some teachers are preferred by administrators, some are liked by the pupils and some taught in classes where there were substantial pupil gains, and generally speaking these were not the same teachers.' In the United Kingdom there have also been studies of supervisors' ratings of teaching. Robertson (1957) asked nineteen supervisors from the same college to rank in order of importance a set of teaching characteristics. Correlations between supervisors ranged from 0·73 to −0·16 and the coefficient of concordance between all supervisors was only 0·38. Brown (1973) asked eighteen supervisors from the same school of education to rate two videotaped lessons on a specially devised rating schedule. All the supervisors rated one lesson better than the other but the intercorrelations of the supervisors' ratings ranged from −0·59 to 0·84. Stones and Morris (1972a) in their survey of the assessment of teaching practice in over 120 institutions in the U.K. found little agreement on the important criteria of teaching. Dress and physical appearance were amongst the most frequently cited criteria and pupil learning was the least frequently mentioned variable. Interestingly enough, Hore (1971) correlated ranked orders of physical attractiveness of women students and their teaching practice marks. The supervisors were men and the correlations were significant. Perhaps thigh length skirts, trouser suits, shoulder length hair or beautiful faces should be regarded as important criteria of teaching . . . Less facetiously, one cannot expect *a priori* that a group of supervisors who may have different teaching experiences would automatically agree on what constitutes good teaching. But if they view videotaped lessons together, discuss their criteria and make them explicit to the trainees then they may achieve consensus at least within the same institution. It was from such discussions that the classroom guidance schedules described in the next Section (p. 61) were derived. One may not agree with the objectives and criteria but at least one knows what they are.

Some teacher educators (for example Taylor, 1973) seem to balk at this approach. They argue that teaching is such a complex and personal activity that we can only achieve the minimal consensus of agreeing to differ. This view has recently been institutionalized in the report of the James committee (1972) which suggests a Pass/Fail system for assessing teaching. The Pass/Fail system is certainly better than using a 15 point scale. For the latter lulls people into thinking that they are objectively assessing good teaching when in fact they are merely grading their own feelings about the students that they are observing. But the Pass/Fail system also has dangers. We must guard against devaluing practical activities simply because assessing them is a complex business. Rather we should strive to discover what we think is good teaching and specify it clearly.

Good and successful?

Good teaching is in the eyes of the beholders. Successful teaching is in the performance of the pupils. Its criteria are gains in pupil learning and these are ostensibly easier to define and measure. Unfortunately there are many roads to successful teaching and the evidence is far from clear-cut (Rosenshine, 1971). Three serious problems bedevil the field. First there are no agreed conceptual or operational definitions of such terms as praise, enthusiasm or criticism. Such conceptions are to some extent culture-bound. 'That's not bad' may be high praise in Northern England, a neutral comment in Southern England and perhaps an insult in New England. Secondly, classroom experiments are difficult to design and carry out and they are rarely directly comparable. Thirdly, pupil learning is not easy to control and measure accurately. This is particularly true of learning in non-mathematical subjects and those with a high value content such as literature. All that one can do in our present state of knowledge is to point tentatively to some findings and suggestively at others. In other words, we have to rely upon making explicit our notions of good teaching and hope that they will be eventually shown to be successful.

Both good and successful teaching are inescapably value-laden, involving, as they do, the selection of criteria and modes of assessment which are shaped by our values. Some values are deeply embedded in our culture and are therefore held by most teachers, some are accepted by groups of us, and some values are predilections of a few individuals. The importance of learning to read, learning to read mathematics and learning to read fifth-century Old Norse are obvious examples. Less obvious but more potent are such social values as learning to help our friends, learning to cooperate with one's leaders and bending the system to one's advantage. But these are not the only causes of distortions of the curriculum or of evaluation procedures. Nor are good and successful synonomous. A teacher may teach his pupils to accurately recite Latin words by applying a rule to their knuckles. Another might control his class with chloroform. Both may be successful, few of us would deem them good teachers. Conversely good teaching may not always be successful. The fashionably 'good' teaching methods of 'learning through discovery' might not be entirely successful with day release apprentices or accountants working for an examination.

The problem of 'good' and 'successful' teaching is nicely highlighted by an experiment of Wittrock (1962). One group of students was told that their educational psychology marks would be based upon the achievement gains of their pupils during block teaching practice. The control group was told that they would be assessed in the conventional way. Pupil achievement tests and measures of their attitudes towards schooling and various academic subjects were administered at the beginning and end of the practice. The achievements of the pupils of the experimental group were significantly greater than those of the control group. But there was a marked decline in the favourable attitudes of the pupils making the most achievement gains. *Who were the successful and who were the good teachers?*

Activity 1

a. List what you consider to be the five most important characteristics of a good teacher and give a positive and a negative instance of the characteristic. An example is given below:

Characteristic	Positive instance 'Good'	Negative instance 'Bad'
Fair mindedness	Tries to help all his pupils	Has favourites

b. Ask a close friend, a colleague, a person of the opposite sex, a primary school pupil and a secondary school pupil to do the exercise given in a.
c. Write a paragraph in which you compare the results of your investigation and indicate your conclusions.
d. What was the single greatest difficulty you encountered whilst actually obtaining the information from your sample? Suggest a reason for this difficulty.

Keep a record of this and subsequent activities in a folder marked Teaching Studies

School experience

Schools are the only place to learn to teach. This has been the assumption underlying most teacher training programmes since college-based demonstration lessons were abandoned forty years ago. Its historical roots are deep. It grew out of the apprenticeship system institutionalized by Joseph Lancaster in the late eighteenth century (Dent, 1971) and it is based upon the notion that a pupil teacher will model himself upon his master. Such a scheme may have been appropriate when pupil teachers worked closely with master teachers and the curriculum and teaching methods were changing slowly. Master teachers were replaced by masters of methods and subsequently by curriculum tutors and teaching practice supervisors. Today most students learn to teach by observing and working with classroom teachers who may not always be experienced or sound exemplars; they may have to rely upon recalled exemplars from their own school days and occasional advice from the class teachers and supervisors.

> Yet so do we preserve at great expense, a vestigial reference to an apprenticeship system, which as far as a tutor and student are concerned in a block practice is long defunct. (Tibble, 1971, p. 104)

The costs are indeed high. There are about 361,000 teachers in post and 120,000* students in training in the U.K. Each of those students occupies a whole class for the equivalent of at least six weeks per year. The 'master' teachers are rarely trained in the techniques of helping others learn to teach. The teaching practice supervisors are often perceived as assessors not guides. They may spend more time travelling to a school than actually observing a student teach, and their school visits have often to be squeezed between lectures and seminars to other groups of students. In the Bristol studies of school experience (Cope, 1971; Brimer and Cope, 1972) the average number of reported visits to schools was one per week. This is barely sufficient for reliable assessment let alone for help and guidance.

Cope's study also reveals other problems of school experience. Students, teachers and supervisors perceive the separate objectives of school experience very differently. Similar results were found by Cohen (1969) in an earlier study. Supervisors and students disagreed on nine out of twelve 'good' approaches to teaching in school. The nine items were:

1. Alternate interesting with less interesting work.
2. Punish the aggressive child for his attacks on other children.
3. Put slow learners with slow learners for all academic work.
4. Interpret 'right' and 'wrong' for the children.
5. Never allow children to know how the teacher will react to classroom situations.
6. Start with strict discipline and gradually become 'approachable'.
7. Allow children to confide in the teacher about personal problems that they may not want to discuss with their parents.

* The D.E.S. are reducing this figure drastically. G.B. 1975.

[14]   8. Give praise sparingly.
        9. Group friends together for Maths and English.

The conditions of school experience vary markedly. Shipman (1965) in a study of a large college found that some students always taught A streams, some never taught A streams; some always had a teacher in the class, some always taught alone; some had more free than teaching time and some had more teaching. Both Shipman and Collier (Collier, 1959) found that teaching practice marks were a partial function of school placements. Put baldly, it is easier to obtain good teaching marks in a girls high school than in a working-class boys secondary school.

As indicated in a previous section, there may be marked disagreements within and between institutions on what constitutes 'good' teaching. Most colleges do not reveal the basis of their assessments to students nor the actual marks received. Feedback from supervisors is often perfunctory and usually unstructured (Stones and Morris, 1972a). Yet without clearly specified criteria of performance and feedback it is difficult to see how one can learn the complex skills of teaching.

Not surprisingly, therefore, there is little rigorous evidence that school experience does train teachers. There is, however, one study which demonstrates that the interaction patterns of students and pupils change during a teaching practice (Wragg, 1972, 1973 – see p. 124–9); and my own studies at Ulster show that supervisors and teachers rated their students on fourteen skill components significantly higher at the end of a term's school experience.

School experience is bedevilled by the problems of placement, organization, objectives and assessment. When working in schools a student is exposed to the interpersonal relations of the staff, he has to learn about the social organization of the school, he has to manage large classes *and* learn to teach. The planning, performance and perception of teaching are in themselves complex activities. It is at least arguable that these central activities should be tackled first. Cope (1971) ends her survey of school experience with the remark that:

> The acquisition by a student of specific skills and techniques . . . instead of being diffused through a block practice might be accelerated by providing a different kind of practice experience. (p. 107)

One such experience is microteaching, which controls the complexity of teaching and which has been shown to be more efficient than school experience in changing teaching behaviours.

Microteaching

Microteaching has been described as a scaled down teaching encounter designed to develop new skills and refine old ones (McKnight, 1971). A trainee (student or teacher) teaches a small group of pupils for five to ten minutes. The lesson is usually videorecorded and subsequently observed and analysed by the trainee with his supervisor.

The original microteaching cycle was developed at Stanford in the early 1960s (Allen
and Ryan, 1969). It consisted of the sequences **Plan – Teach – Observe (Critique) –
Replan – Reteach – Reobserve**. Each cycle was devoted to the practice of one component skill such as set and closure (the beginning and ending of lesson segments),
effective questioning, pupil reinforcement and pupil participation. Lectures and skill
demonstrations were given to the students prior to the practice of the skill. There are
now many variations on the original Stanford model (Ward, 1970; Borg, 1970). The
model used at the New University of Ulster is **Plan – Teach – Observe**. Emphasis is
given to planning and perception as well as performance skills. The programme is
carried out in teams of three or four students working with a supervisor. This is more
economical than the Stanford model. It enables students to plan their lessons together,
to teach linked themes if they wish to, to observe each other's teaching and to discuss
it. The loss of the *immediate* reteach is more than offset by these gains. Immediate reteach
scores at Ulster were almost always lower than teach scores and students disliked the
reteach sessions (Brown and Gibbs, 1974).

The microteaching format satisfies the requirements of the teacher training model
(p. 9). Rules of planning are given in lectures and seminars, performance is split into
its component skills and the skills are demonstrated, opportunities for practice are given
in controlled conditions. Feedback in the form of videorecordings is given in supervisory
sessions and students are taught what cues to look for in their interaction with pupils.
The system is augmented by the use of rating schedules, checklists and interaction
analyses. These focus the student's and supervisor's attention upon the skill under review.
On a *priori* grounds one would therefore expect microteaching to be more efficient
than school experience. Does experimental evidence confirm this view?

We can examine this question by looking at the relationship between performance
in microteaching and school experience, microteaching compared with school experience and the changes which occur during microteaching.

Table 1 sets out a sample of studies which compare scores obtained in microteaching
and school experience. All the experiments cited used rating schedules and trained
observers of teaching.

Table 1. Microteaching and school experience

Source	Sample	Significance level	Statistical test
Aubertine (1964)	30 students	$P < 0.001$	Chi-square
Allen and Fortune (1966)	60 students	$P < 0.001$	Chi-square
Allen and Fortune (1966)	114 students	$P < 0.01$	Chi-Square
Kallenbach and Gall (1969)	27 students	$P < 0.01$	Correlation ($r = 0.51$)
Brown (1973)	34 students	$P < 0.01$	Correlation ($r = 0.84$)

The first three studies were carried out at Stanford. Grades of A and B were taken
as the criterion of effectiveness. In the first study six students were rated considerably

lower than their peers, and of these five failed to meet the criterion. In the second study, three of the five lowest scoring students on microteaching did not meet the criterion on school experience and two students predicted to meet the criterion did not. In the third study, microteaching scores were related to performance in the first month of full-time teaching. Two unsatisfactory lessons out of three were taken as failure to meet the criterion. Eleven of the lowest scoring twelve students did not meet the criterion in school. Two of the top twelve microteaching students also did not meet the criterion. In the fourth study correlations were obtained between microteaching scores and scores on school experience nine months later. In the fifth study the gap between microteaching and school experience scores was fifteen months. In none of these studies did the school experience observers know the microteaching scores of the students.

Such studies clearly point to a strong relationship between microteaching and school experience. Microteaching performance in fact appears to be the best predictor we have of performance in the classroom. In contrast, correlations between personality or intelligence and school experience scores rarely rise above 0·2 (Garner, 1973). But correlations only tell us that students who are good at microteaching are also good at classroom teaching. They do not tell us anything about the effects of the training programme. In the fifth study cited (Brown, 1973) an attempt to overcome this criticism was made. The score of each of eight microteaching cycles was related to the school experience score. A multiple stepwise regression analysis was performed to find the best predictor of the school experience score. It was the score of the final microteaching cycle of the term, thus suggesting that the cumulative effect of microteaching had an effect upon the students' performance in classrooms. Incidentally, the obtained multiple regression equation of microteaching scores accurately predicted 31 out of the 34 students' final scores in school experience.

But multiple regression analyses do not always satisfy the statistically unsophisticated. They might prefer a direct comparison between students who had been trained by microteaching methods and by school experience methods. Only two teams of experimenters have attempted this task – the tangle of uncontrolled variables in such studies is daunting. Allen and Fortune (1966) compared the performance of students who spent one hour per day for fifteen days in microteaching laboratories with those who had three weeks of teaching normal classes in schools. The criterion was performance in a microteaching lesson rated by independent observers. Kallenbach and Gall (1969) replicated this experiment but their criterion was performance in classrooms two months and nine months later. In both experiments the results marginally favoured the microteaching group. The pay-off was that microteaching achieved these results in one-fifth of the time; it used considerably fewer pupils; it was easier to organize; and the system was under the control of the course organizers. Similar results have also been found with teachers on vacation in-service courses (Pinney and Dodge, 1970). The more interesting question is: How does a student's performance change during microteaching?

The studies at Stanford (Fortune, Cooper and Allen, 1967; Cooper and Stroud, 1967) of over two hundred students found significant improvements in planning, clarity of explanations, use of pupil ideas and positive reinforcement. Supervisors, high school pupils and independent observers rated first and last microlessons on a specially devised rating schedule known as the Stanford Teacher Competence Appraisal Guide (see Stones and Morris, 1972). This experiment was replicated twice at Ulster and, in addition, self ratings, peer ratings and analyses of teacher–pupil interactions were carried out. The students themselves, the supervisors and the independent observers all detected improvements in performance. The interaction analyses revealed significant changes on nineteen out of thirty variables. Of these, the most important were:

> At the end of the programme, students asked fewer questions but received correspondingly more answers.
> The pupil answers were longer.
> The students were more fluent (the gaps of silence in teacher talk were fewer), they used pupil reinforcement and the pupils' ideas more frequently, they lectured less and their pupils made more voluntary contributions to the discussions.

Despite this and other related evidence reviewed elsewhere (McAleese and Unwin, 1971; Brown, 1973) there are still a few critics who view microteaching and similar approaches with suspicion (Andrews, 1971). Their main fear appears to be that microteaching will produce homogenized teachers with standard smiles and procedures. A subsidiary fear is that the skills may not be internalized. The first rests on the assumption that microteaching is *too* effective, the second that it is not at all effective. Truth, as usual, holds the middle ground. Microteaching will help you to sharpen and develop your teaching skills, it will help you to eliminate gross errors and it will build up your confidence. It will not change your personality overnight, it will not solve all your teaching problems. It will not make you into a brilliant gifted teacher – just a better one.

Recommended reading

STONES, E. and MORRIS, S. (1972) *Teaching Practice: Problems and Perspectives*, Methuen. This is the first text to deal systematically with new approaches to the training of teachers. It describes in more detail the rationale underlying school experience and microteaching. It also contains an excellent discussion of interaction analysis and simulation, and reprints of important papers.

Section Two

The teaching skills programme

Units I, II	*Planning*
Units III, IV	*Perception*
Units V, VI, VII	*Performance*

Introduction

The next six units are concerned with improving your planning, perception and performance of teaching skills. Units I and II deal with planning lessons and concept teaching, units III and IV with perceiving teaching and units V, VI and VII with exposition, questioning and discussion skills. To gain the maximum from the programme you should tackle every activity in the order they are given. You should videotape your lessons or, less preferably, audiotape them. Full details on how to set up a microteaching laboratory and programme will be given in Section Three.

The pupils you teach may be small groups of children or, if this is not convenient, your peers. Children, aged eight or over, have been taught in microteaching settings. Even the youngest age group can significantly discriminate between untrained and trained teachers. Children's comments on a person's teaching skills are often perceptive and remarkably illuminating. Peer teaching has some advantages in the initial stages of planning and perceiving. All the participants then experience what it is like to be a pupil and they can discuss the microlessons from this standpoint. Effective questioning, pupil reinforcement and participation are probably best tackled with children as pupils.

As far as possible, microteaching should be undertaken in teams of three or four students or teachers. This facilitates lesson planning and perception and enables the team to work on linked themes if they wish. Whilst one person teaches, the others may operate the VTR equipment and observe the teacher and pupils. The order in which the members of the team teach should be rotated. Discussions during the critique sessions should focus sharply and *constructively* upon the particular skill under review. You will probably want to watch the whole of your first and last teaching performance in the programme. It is not necessary to observe the whole of the other performances. The time saved may be usefully spent in open friendly discussion of ways of improving your skills. Further details of these points are given in the succeeding units.

Unit I · Planning teaching

The first two units of the teaching skills programme are devoted to the planning of lessons and concept teaching. On reading the first unit you should be able to distinguish between educational and instructional objectives; to write specific instructional objectives and to carry out elementary topic analyses. On completing the second unit you will be able to set out a microlesson plan and apply your knowledge of lesson planning to the teaching of concepts, you will have taught at least one microlesson on a concept and you may be able to identify some important characteristics of your own concept teaching. Some suggestions for further reading and answers are given at the end of unit II.

The units are designed for beginners in teaching. Unit I is probably the most difficult one (and some would say the least enjoyable) in the whole programme. Do not skip it. Planning is a vital element in teaching. Systematic planning almost always yields better results in teaching (Peck and Tucker, 1973; Waimon, 1972). It leaves you free to monitor the class's performance and it reduces the likelihood of problems of control. The ease with which an accomplished teacher steers his way through a series of lessons is probably due to the attention he devoted to planning and organization in his early years of teaching. In terms of the teaching model on page 9, he has developed and internalized rules of planning. The rules in this unit and the following one are intended as a guide in the initial stages of teaching. Once you have mastered them, you should develop your own approach to planning. As a matter of fact, in mastering them you will develop your own approach.

The relationship between planning, performance and perception in a lesson is set out in Figure 4. At first glance all planning occurs before the lesson and all perception during the viewing session and after teaching. A moment's reflection may convince you that some modification in your plan will occur during the lesson as a result of your perceptions of the pupils' responses. How far you allow the pupils' interests and responses to modify your original intentions and plans is a question of value. An extremely child-centred teacher might insist that the children's immediate needs and interests should shape the lesson. This requires considerable mastery of the curriculum

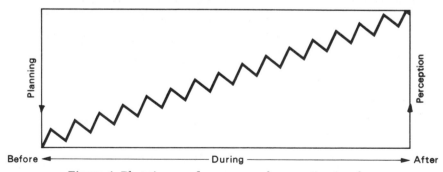

Figure 4. Planning, performance and perception in a lesson

content and an intimate knowledge of the pupils. During the early stages of this teaching programme I suggest you should set yourself modest objectives and try to stick fairly close to them. As your repertoire of skills and knowledge increases you can move off this base to more heady heights. Premature attempts at high level teaching or mountaineering lead to hidden, sometimes buried, failures.

Discussion of Activity 2

Activity 2 may have been mildly nerve racking – even though you were working with cooperative peers. They are not likely to have suffered psychological damage from your first fumbling attempts. Before teaching the microlesson you may have felt that ten minutes is not sufficient to teach any topic; that you could not teach your peers because you did not know how much they knew about the topic; that you did not know what to do; that the camera would affect your performance and that the situation was too artificial. You may add further rationalizations to this list – and then consider the formidable task of teaching the same topic to forty real pupils.

The situation was deliberately unstructured, simplified and artificial. Most of you probably forgot about the camera after the first few minutes of teaching. You were not expected to know precisely what to do – but it is hoped that you recognize the need to learn. The entering behaviours of pupils (what they know already) is a problem you will learn to cope with on this course. Most segments of teaching activities are less than ten minutes in duration. If you could not teach your topic, it was either too big or you taught it inefficiently. Teachers rarely have enough time in any course to do all they want to do. They sometimes assume that because they know a great deal about a topic that they must transmit all this knowledge to their pupils. A more worthwhile approach is to ask what do the pupils need to know at this stage of their development. The next section on lesson planning touches on this issue.

Lesson planning

The last section of Activity 2 asked you to give honest answers to six questions on your planning. These questions are presented in modified form below. They are central to the planning of lessons and courses. This section of the unit looks at each question in a little more detail. The activities are designed to steer you through the complex labyrinth of planning. When you have completed them you will find the next unit on planning microlessons straightforward.

Key questions in planning

1. What kinds of things do you want the pupils to learn? (Skills, facts, concepts, attitudes, values)
2 What are your precise instructional objectives?
3. What is the most appropriate sequence of topics and tasks?

Activity 2

Your first teaching assignment

Before reading about lesson planning in the following pages you should try a few preliminary teaching moves with your peers.

Plan a ten minute lesson on any topic of your choice which may be of interest to your team of peers. Teach and videorecord it.

One of the team should signal to you at about the eighth minute so you can bring your lesson to a close. Assume that at the tenth minute the school bell has rung and your pupils must leave immediately for their next class.

When all members of the team have completed their teaching tasks you should proceed to the next section of the assignment.

Just before viewing the lesson with your peers you should tell them what you intended that they should learn. (What children learn, remember, is the essence of teaching.)

If you have not seen yourself on videotape before you will be fascinated by your own mannerisms, body shape and movements as well as your teaching performance and the reactions of your pupils. During viewing you should follow your natural inclinations to look closely at yourself. Psychologists have dubbed this phenomenon the auto-elic response or the 'cosmetic effect' (How do I look?). Whilst looking try to decide which mannerisms are socially acceptable and which you think should be changed. Stroking one's chin when asked a question is socially acceptable, shoving a finger up your nostril is probably not.
After viewing you should tell the group what you thought of your mannerisms and your teaching. Indicate what you consider to be your good points, the mistakes you made and how you might improve. You should then ask your team members to comment on your performance in relation to your expressed intentions and to put forward suggestions to improve your performance. If a supervisor is present, he should confine himself to prompting, asking questions which lead to self evaluation and summarizing the group's views at the end of the critique sessions. Further details on the suggested role of the supervisor are given in the final section of the book (p. 139 et seq).

A day or so later the team should again meet. You should read each other's lesson notes before re-viewing the lessons. Whilst re-viewing them ask yourself these questions — and answer them honestly.

> What kinds of things did I want the pupils to learn?
> Did I really know what I intended to teach?
> Did I have an order of tasks and topics in mind when I planned and taught my lesson?
> Did I have a method of teaching in mind?
> What did the group of 'pupils' learn from me?
> How do I know that they learnt these things?

Keep your original lesson notes (in your Teaching Studies folder) and the videorecording for use later in the course.

4. What are the most appropriate methods?
    5. How should the teaching and learning be evaluated?

What kinds of things do you want your pupils to learn?

The psychological contents of learning may be described as psychomotor, cognitive or affective. We teach children to play sport and to handle tools and machinery. We teach them to recall facts, solve problems and think critically. We shape their attitudes towards learning in general and subjects in particular. We do this through what we teach and how we teach it. The three content areas or domains are enshrined in Bloom's *Taxonomy of Educational Objectives* (Bloom, 1956) which was designed for assessing test items. The precise relationship between the domains would lead us into a discussion of the nature of man which is vital, interesting and unlikely to be solved before you are working in schools. Bloom also specified levels within each domain. These may be of some value to course designers (but see Sockett, 1971; Pring, 1971), they may not be useful to beginners. For the moment you should stick to the triad of psychomotor, cognitive and affective domains.

Educational and instructional objectives

Most beginners and some experienced teachers respond to the question 'What were you trying to do in that lesson?' with answers such as 'I was teaching them algebra' or 'I was teaching them about Hamlet'. Lofty idealists and con-men might reply to the question with 'I was developing their aesthetic sensibilities'. Such aims are laudable and we should reflect upon them from time to time. They are, however, long term and diffuse and they cannot be nailed firmly to specific teaching episodes or pupil behaviours. We call such long term aims *educational objectives*. Aims which specify precisely what we intend the pupils to learn in a lesson or course are labelled *instructional objectives*. When these aims can be expressed in terms of observable pupil behaviour we speak of *explicit* instructional objectives. Aims which are expressed only in terms of inner changes in the pupils we speak of as *implicit* instructional objectives. Generally speaking, explicit instructional objectives are preferable for they allow us to evaluate the success of the teaching and so to improve upon it.

Nonetheless, some teachers of English (see Stenhouse, 1971) object to the use of explicit instructional objectives. The point out that teaching is a subtle interpersonal process; that whatever they teach, their pupils will each take away something different; that sensitivity cannot be reduced to lists of objectives and that responses to literature are complex, unique activities which cannot easily be categorized.

Despite such remarks, most English teachers do distinguish good work from bad, they can detect improvement in reading, writing and responses to literature, and presumably they know what they hope their pupils will achieve in a course of study. It follows from this that explicit instructional objectives may be written for many aspects of English teaching. This is not to say that the objectives should be as detailed or as tightly knit as those currently used by scientists. Nor is it a denial of the subtleties of teaching. [25] It is precisely because teaching is a complex process that we need objectives to highlight and communicate the essential features of what we are doing. Perhaps the root of their objections to objectives is the language of behavioural scientists rather than the task of specifying one's intentions.

Before deciding your views on these matters, you are asked to try the methods proposed in this unit. The task of writing instructional objectives will at least help you to clarify your teaching problems.

Activity 3

Which of the following are *best described as* educational objectives, explicit instructional objectives and implicit instructional objectives? Jot down a reason for your answer.

a. To solve simultaneous equations.
b. To appreciate the significance of Hamlet.
c. To walk upon the beam from one end to the other whilst being watched by the remainder of the class.
d. To understand trigonometry.
e. To develop an unprejudiced attitude towards Catholics.
f. To value tolerance.
g. To change the pupil's perceptions of the paintings of Picasso.
h. To play cricket.
i. To develop the capacity to enjoy leisure.
j. To socialize children into the society in which they are born.
k. To teach pupils the principles of democracy.

Answers are given at the end of the book (p. 145)

Explicit instructional objectives

Activity 3 was designed to promote inner cerebral changes – to make you think. Most of the *instructional* objectives were taken from the first lesson notes written by a group of students for Activity 2. Your difficulty in classifying their objectives was due to their lack of specificity. When writing explicit instructional objectives you need to specify:

(i) What the pupils will be able to do at the end of the lesson or course (known as their terminal behaviour).

(ii) The important conditions under which the performance will occur.

(iii) The criteria of performance — how it will be observed and, perhaps, measured.

Only one item in Activity 3 meets these criteria. Which is it? (Answer, page 145)

One's first attempts at writing objectives often yield implicit objectives. These may often be changed into explicit objectives by simply changing the verbs. To understand, to grasp (the essential features), to appreciate, to think are implicit verbs. 'To *understand* trigonometry' may be translated into the explicit instructional objective, 'By the end of the course all the pupils *will be able to solve six* simple problems which require the use of sine, cosine or tangent and the appropriate trigonometrical tables.'

Notice how translating implicit into explicit objectives forces you to spell out more clearly what you intend the pupils to learn, the conditions of learning, and how you propose to observe or measure their performance. By clearly specifying explicit instructional objectives you go a long way towards choosing the appropriate resources and methods. Herein lies the importance of the next five activities.

Writing instructional objectives

We come now to the most difficult part of the lesson planning, the writing of instructional objectives. There are two pitfalls : vagueness and over specificity. The gap between them is narrow so proceed cautiously. Behavioural scientists sometimes overreact to the dangers of the former and humanities-based specialists to the dangers of the latter. To borrow a metaphor, vagueness and over specificity are like mists and trees, they both prevent you from seeing the shape of the forest. To get a clear picture of the instructional sequence you need to translate relatively vague objectives into concise and fairly precise explicit objectives. Implicit objectives are translatable into a variety of explicit objectives which are appropriate for different sets of pupils. It is possible to teach Hamlet to seven- or seventeen-year-olds. Precisely how and what you teach about Hamlet is built into the expected changes in pupil learning given in your explicit objectives. In this way you are taking into account the levels of mastery and experience of your pupils. If you are expecting several changes in any one lesson you are probably being over-ambitious or over-precise. If you cannot indicate clearly how you will observe (or measure) the pupil's learning you are probably being too vague.

Activity 4

Identifying explicit instructional objectives

Set out below is a list of instructional objectives and a set of criteria for examining them. Place a √ in the column if the objective meets the criterion and a × if it does not.

The answers are given at the end of the book (p. 145).

	Criteria for examining objectives				
	Identifies desired behaviour	Explicitly describes what learner will do	Describes conditions under which performance will occur	Expected behaviour can be observed	Expected behaviour can be evaluated

The learner will:

a. Write his name.
b. Understand nation interdependence.
c. Count accurately when playing classroom number games.
d. Identify and classify the propaganda devices used in syndicated columns on the editorial page of the local paper (based on structure developed in class).
e. Sing the correct words when the national anthem is played in school assemblies.
f. Know his full name and address when asked by the teacher.
g. As a player, be honest in calling tennis shots falling near the line.
h. Name the planets of the solar system in order — from the sun — when asked by the teacher.
i. Identify relevant element in mathematic word problems when extraneous data are included.
j. Have a better understanding of the federal system of checks and balances.
k. Name six carnivorous animals.
l. Swim the length of the school pool in less than one minute, without artificial support, starting from an immersed position at the deep end of the pool.
m. Think clearly when called upon in class to think on his feet.
n. Respond orally and accurately to multiplication flash cards from $1 \times 1 = \ldots$ through $12 \times 12 = \ldots$, when cards are presented to him in class.
o. Cover his mouth every time he sneezes.

Topics and their sequence (topic analysis)

A clear specification of explicit instructional objectives will help you to identify the important topic for your pupils and the logical order, if any, of the topics. The order in which you actually present the tasks to the pupils is partly determined by the teaching methods you adopt. These are dealt with in the next section. Your first task analysis is drawn from the most logical of all subjects, mathematics.

Activity 5

Writing explicit objectives

Translate the following objectives into explicit instructional objectives. Only one explicit objective for each given objective is required. Check your explicit objectives against the first four criteria given in Activity 4 (identifies desired behaviour; explicitly describes what the learner will do; describes conditions under which performance will occur; expected behaviour can be observed).

Some possible answers are given at the end of the book (p. 145).

Given implicit objective	*An explicit instructional objective*
The pupils will:	By the end of the teaching episode (microlesson, set of microlessons, lesson, lessons) the pupil will be able to:

1. Understand simple French.
2. Understand simple equations.
3. Know about Hamlet.
4. Know how to debate.
5. Know the difference between poetry and prose.
6. Understand the rules of chess.
7. Appreciate the works of Van Gogh.
8. Understand the geography of his neighbourhood.
9. Understand the laws of reflection.
10. Know how to prepare hydrochloric acid.
11. Grasp the significance of the American Civil War.
12. Appreciate the importance of maternal care for young children.

Activity 6

Put in an ascending order of difficulty the following simple equations.

a. $2x - 3 = 5$

b. $3x = 9$

c. $x + 5 = 8$

d. $3 + x = 9$

e. $12 = 2x$

f. $14 = 3c + 5$

g. $2x + 4 = 10$

h. $\frac{1}{3}x = 5$

i. $\frac{3}{4}x + 2 = 8$

j $\frac{2}{3}x = 4$

Activity 7

One of your peers should be asked to sharpen a blunt pencil with a penknife. Observe his actions closely whilst he does it and then, with your peers, design a short training programme to teach a normal adult to sharpen a pencil. Describe the resources you require, write a precise explicit instructional objective indicating the conditions under which you expect the learning to take place and specify the criteria of the trainee's terminal behaviour — your measure of successful completion of the test. Write out the instructions for each sub-task in the order in which you think they should occur.

   The resources required and instructions should then be read out to the 'trainee' who should then attempt to carry them out. The training programme should then be modified where necessary. Then try the modified programme with a peer playing the part of a child who has never seen a pencil, penknife or pencil sharpening. You may assume the 'child' has adequate psychomotor skills for the task.

Discussion of Activity 6

Discerning readers will have noted the instruction 'Put in *an* ascending order . . .' Most of you will have placed (b) or (c) as the easiest item and (f), (g), (i),)j) as the most difficult items. Disagreements are likely to occur about the relative difficulty of (c) or (d) and (f) or (g). Pupils usually find (d) type harder than (c) and (g) harder than (f). The items (f), (g) are regarded as more difficult because they are made up of subtopics exemplified by (e), (b), (c) and (d).

Which items (subtopics) are contained in i)?

Discussion of Activity 7

Then pencil sharpening activity was used to teach you to specify terminal behaviours. This activity was also chosen to illustrate the importance of specifying clear instructions in the correct order. You may have found the exercise difficult – particularly the second part of teaching a 'child' to sharpen a pencil. Many sets of instructions which we use in classrooms and laboratories are at least as complicated. For example:

1. In mathematics: Constructing diagrams, bisecting lines and angles, carrying out complicated calculations, applying formulae to problems.
2. In science: Setting up and carrying out simple experiments. Drawing and labelling apparatus.
3. In environmental studies: Drawing and labelling maps, learning to calculate heights and distances from map contours.
4. In creative arts: Learning the basic skills of basketry, pottery and model building.
5. In English: Analysing the structure of sentences. Examining the rhyming pattern of a poem.

What are the most appropriate methods?

One can distinguish four main pedagogical strategies or methods of teaching. They may, for convenience, be labelled lecturing (or exposition), discussion, guided discovery, and open discovery. They may be and are used at all levels in education from the nursery school to the graduate seminar. Before hotly disputing this point you should read further.

LECTURING AND DISCUSSION TECHNIQUES

Lecturing has been humorously described as the art of transferring information from the lecturer's notebooks to the student's notebook without passing through the heads of either. In fact, lecturing consists of narrating, describing and explaining. The lecture may be predominantly oral. It may include writing on a board or overhead projector. Skills, concepts, facts and values may be taught in this way. The activity is teacher centred and interaction is minimal. Experiments described by McCleish (1968), McKeachie (1963) and Beard (1973) indicate that immediate recall of information from formal lectures by university and college students is usually between 30 and 40 per cent. The formal lecture is not renowned for its effectiveness in teaching psychomotor skills or promoting attitude change.

These findings contribute to the fashionable ideology of dismissing lecturing and [31] formal teaching as old-fashioned (and therefore bad) and inefficient. They are often, illogically, taken as support for other methods of teaching. Excessive use of any one method of teaching is likely to be ineffective and dull. On the bright side, lecturing with enthusiasm (Rosenshine, 1970) does lead to higher pupil achievement and more favourable attitudes than lecturing without enthusiasm. In almost all lessons or learning sequences the teacher has to present information and ideas. He has to introduce topics, set the scene for new learning, summarize the main points of the learning activity and inspire and stimulate further learning. All of these activities require the use of lecturing techniques – at various points in a learning sequence. It is not so much the lecture as its length which produces discouraging results. Unfortunately we have no clear-cut evidence on the appropriate length of a lecturing episode in a lesson or the frequency with which they should occur. They can, as yet, only be determined *in situ*. A useful rule of thumb is that a lecturing episode without any pupil participation should not exceed 10 per cent of a lesson with a class of fourteen-year-old secondary children. The duration of lecturing episodes should be correspondingly shorter for younger children. It may be longer for older children. The exception is story telling which may be longer – but it should satisfy the pupils' needs and interests as much as the teacher's dramatic predilections.

Discussion consists of questions, answers and comments by both teachers and pupils. Since it involves feedback and pupil participation one would expect it to be an effective method of learning. The research evidence bears this out (McKeachie, 1963 ; Abercrombie, 1971). It is particularly useful for helping pupils to solve complex problems or to carry out complicated tasks. It is a useful preliminary or follow up to any independent learning. It is, however, a relatively slow method of learning and lengthy discussions can lead to restlessness and frustration. There is no clear-cut evidence which suggests when to use discussion techniques and how long this should last. Most lessons should contain some discussion; lengthy discussions should be reserved for important complex problems or value questions; discussion classes should be monitored and drawn to a close *before* the student or pupil interest in the subject has waned and pupils or students should be taught how to discuss. Further details on lecturing and discussion techniques are given in subsequent units.

DISCOVERY METHODS

Discovery methods may be placed upon a continuum, from the highly structured to the completely open ended. In discovery methods the objectives are *deliberately* hidden from the pupils until they have completed the task. A teacher is operating at the highly structured end of the continuum when he gives a clear set of instructions which result in pupils apparently discovering a fact, idea or skill for themselves. The extreme of the open ended situation is when a teacher abnegates his role and lets the children discover whatever they wish. The middle range consists of devising learning situations based upon directions and questions which give the pupils freedom to explore different possibilities and solutions to problems. (See De Cecco, 1968, for a description of these methods.) Lecturing and discussion merge into guided discovery which in its turn becomes open ended discovery. The location of the transition points are a nice conceptual problem for devotees of linguistic philosophy. It need not concern us. The efficacy of the methods are of interest. Wittrock (1966) and Cronbach (1966) indicate that open discovery methods are not particularly effective at generating pupil learning. Perhaps what the researchers measured was not what the pupil learnt. Carefully structured discovery methods have a long history (Socrates circa 469–399 B.C.) and a promising future. The methods are based upon the nature of insight learning and curiosity. But they can be time consuming. One has to balance the costs of using discovery techniques against the pay-offs for the pupil. Excessive use of discovery techniques for low level learning may evoke 'Oh, not again. Why doesn't he just tell us?'

The subsequent units of this book do not describe discovery methods in detail. I do describe effective questioning which is an integral part of guided discovery and elements of the chapters on presentation and participation are also relevant. Wide open discovery approaches are ignored – they have more in common with non-directive counselling and T-group training than teaching. Students interested in the use of such techniques in the classroom should consult Grainger's (1970) description of 'you can say what you like and just about do what you like' and Simon Stuart's (1969) text on English teaching.

So far this section has been concerned with teaching methods. Each has its costs and pay-offs. So you must choose the appropriate mix of methods for your instructional objectives and the particular set of pupils you are teaching and, if you are microteaching, for the skills you are practising. Guided discovery would be an inappropriate vehicle for practising teacher explanation, and exposition would be inappropriate for practising reinforcement techniques.

We come now to a cluster of variables which may be labelled teaching styles. These are ways in which a teacher handles the teaching methods and they may be as important as the methods themselves. It is possible to lecture, discuss and use guided discovery methods in a lively, friendly and well organized way. It is also possible to use any of these methods in a dull, boring, cold, hostile way. Different teaching styles engender different socio-emotional climates. Some examples of these are given in the next unit. The notion of 'good' teaching (see Section One, p. 10–12) usually includes the establishment of friendly democratic relationships. In practice this may not be easy to achieve. The pupils may have other intentions and expectations of their teachers. It may be better to base one's initial attempts at teaching upon the pupil's expectancies. This may involve the use of authority-centred strategies and styles. Put less gingerly, it may involve being tough.

Evaluating teaching in microlessons

Teachers and pupils live together in crowded places for six hours per day for 180 days per year. The crowd of pupils slowly becomes a group with distinctive patterns of interac-

tion and norms (Hargreaves, 1967; Lacey, 1970). The teacher is therefore faced with
problems of communication and control – and so are the pupils. He and the pupils
are under constant surveillance of each other. They interpret each other's actions and
each creates his own picture of the reality of classroom life. The teacher categorizes
and learns about his pupils. The pupils often intuitively know what their teacher and
fellow pupils think of their abilities and aspirations (Nash, 1973). In short, evaluation
of teaching and learning is an ongoing process in the classroom.

This description may not match your expectations of the subject of evaluation for
it begins with where the action is – in the classroom not the examination hall. In
Section 1 (p. 6) I distinguished between long-term evaluation and monitoring. A detailed
description of the subtleties of item writing, test construction and the setting and marking
of essays would take us too far afield. Unit VI (Effective Questioning) and the suggestions
for further reading at the end of the next unit contain relevant information. It is possible
to measure pupil achievement in microteaching but this is only feasible in research
projects (MacClennan, 1974). This section is concerned only with a few simple points
on immediate evaluation or monitoring in microteaching situations and some strategies
to adopt to improve your teaching.

During most teaching episodes or microlessons you should try to find out what your
pupils have learnt by setting the pupils specific tasks and asking them specific questions,
observing them at work and monitoring their non-verbal behaviour. Pupils who sit
back in their chairs with a glazed look in their eyes may have just experienced puzzle-
ment, bewilderment or total incomprehension. Watch out for these signals when pupils
are also working on a topic or project. Approach and ask them if they know what
to do. If they answer 'yes' ask them to explain it to you. If their explanation is a good
one you can then use it with other pupils. If it is not, re-explain in simple language.
If their answer is 'no', either ask another pupil to explain, or explain the idea or task
in simpler language than you first used. If the same pupil frequently does not understand
in a set of lessons, you should direct your questions towards him during class discussion –
preferably in a relaxed, friendly manner. 'Now, John, can you tell us what we've got
to do?' is more effective than barking 'John. Have you been listening?' If the majority
of the class does not understand, it is better to leave the topic and return to it after
you have rethought and replanned it. Spontaneous elaboration by a teacher can often
confuse children even more. If it is absolutely impossible to leave the topic then you
should ask the children to stop whatever they are doing. Settle them down – 'Now
(Pause) I want you to listen very carefully . . .' Explain again simply. Ask some of
the pupils questions about the topic. Summarize their answers in their language and
then again check that they have understood.

After each microlesson you should immediately jot down your impressions of your
performance and pupil learning in relation to your objectives. Further details are given
in the next unit.

Finally, let me emphasize that evaluation in microteaching is concerned with improving your teaching skills. If the pupils do not learn, the fault often lies in ourselves,
the objectives we set and not in our pupils.

The previous unit ranged over the field of planning. This was a necessary preliminary to microplanning just as microplanning is a necessary preliminary to microteaching.

During the early stages of microteaching you may have some difficulty in specifying your objectives – let alone matching performance and pupil learning against them. As a matter of fact, we are often not clear what our precise objectives are until after we have taught, viewed and thought over for the first time. This is particularly true in wide ranging fields such as English teaching. It is therefore worthwhile looking for the hidden as well as the intended objectives in your microlesson. Hidden objectives may, at first glance, seem a contradictory term. It has been chosen to emphasize that sometimes we are not conscious of all of our intentions until we have completed a task. It is preferred to 'unintended outcomes' for these may be not intended, not consciously intended but later recognized as an intention (hidden objective), or intended to *not* occur. Needless to say the relationships of objectives, intentionality and consciousness of intent is a nice conceptual problem for philosophers of education. For the moment, stick to the framework of 'hidden objectives'. Later on you can reject it if you wish. Jot down on your lesson plan after viewing your microlesson so that you gradually build up a repertoire of objectives and topics. This eventually will make your planning easier and more effective.

Figure 5 summarizes the main features of the planning cycle. Topics and methods are placed together because most people find it easier to think of these together. The cycle gives you a guide to your planning and viewing of lessons. On page 36 there is a planning lesson record. Note that you are asked to briefly record your impressions before viewing and again afterwards. This helps to sharpen perceptions of your own teaching so that eventually you may find that the videotape merely confirms what you already know and feel about your performance and the pupils' learning. This is followed by samples of lesson planning records by students. You might like to compare these. On page 42 you will find a set of possible pupil activities. This is often a neglected feature of student teachers' plans.

If you are viewing a videotape of your lesson, you should look at your lesson plan, your notes and the component skill guide before the playback. During playback pay particular attention to the component skill under review and then *briefly* consider how far you achieved your objectives. The component skill guides are described in units III to VII.

Figure 5. The planning cycle

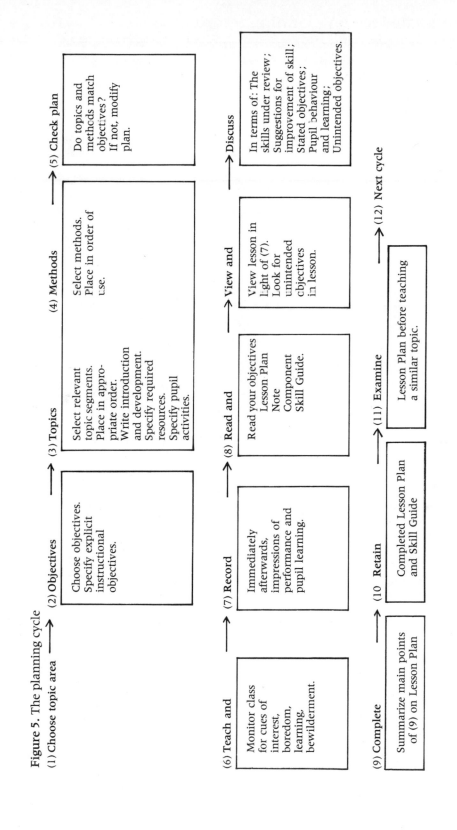

(1) Choose topic area →

(2) Objectives →

Choose objectives. Specify explicit instructional objectives.

(3) Topics →

Select relevant topic segments. Place in appropriate order. Write introduction and development. Specify required resources. Specify pupil activities.

(4) Methods →

Select methods. Place in order of use.

(5) Check plan

Do topics and methods match objectives? If not, modify plan.

→ Discuss

In terms of: The skills under review; Suggestions for improvement of skill; Stated objectives; Pupil behaviour and learning; Unintended objectives.

→ (12) Next cycle

(6) Teach and

Monitor class for cues of interest, boredom, learning, bewilderment.

↑ (7) Record

Immediately afterwards, impressions of performance and pupil learning.

↑ (8) Read and

Read your objectives Lesson Plan Note Component Skill Guide.

→ View and

View lesson in light of (7). Look for unintended objectives in lesson.

(9) Complete

Summarize main points of (9) on Lesson Plan

↑ (10 Retain

Completed Lesson Plan and Skill Guide

↑ (11) Examine

Lesson Plan before teaching a similar topic.

An annotated lesson planning record

Name: Topic area: Class: Date:

Skill/s under review: /Global   Time:

Note on pupils' knowledge, if known:

1. Explicit objective/s

- These objectives refer to the pupils' learning. Your learning to teach objectives are specified in the rating schedules. You should read them before planning, teaching or observing your lessons. CHECK: Do they explicitly describe what the pupil may learn, the conditions of learning, and the criteria being used? Are they predominantly psychomotor, effective or cognitive?

2. Topic/method

- Lecture? Discussion? Guided discovery?

a) Introduction:

b) Development:

                                    - CHECK: Does the sequencing of the topic and method/s selected seem appropriate?

                                    Will you have available all the material resources you need? e.g. Blackboard, charts, overhead projector, apparatus, pupil-learning materials?

c) Completion:

                                    Are the pupils doing a sufficiently wide variety of activities?

d) Resources:

e) Pupil activities:

3. Post-lesson impression

- This should include your impression of a) pupil behaviour and learning; b) your performance; c) any main digression from your objective/s

4. Post-viewing impression

- This should take into account a) performance of skill/s under review (and suggested ways of improving upon them); b) stated objectives; c) pupil behavioural learning in relation to b); hidden objectives and pupil learning. NOTE: The discussion after viewing should focus on the skills. The other items should arise out of this rather than the reverse. Include a comment on any substantial digression from your objective/s. Estimate whether it was justified.

reader# A student's lesson planning records

A student's first attempt at a lesson planning record

effort*Time:* 15 minutes — Taken with pupils

Topic: Coleraine area. To learn the location of the main physical features of Coleraine, the growth of new housing, the social geography of the area. The pupils will be asked to draw maps and illustrations.

I will use a blackboard map and a 3D model, showing the river and bridge. Then I'll ask the children to name different parts of Coleraine and write them on their maps, and to say what they notice about the streets at the bridge (they all converge on the bridge). I'll then ask them questions about the lesson.

Post-viewing impression: I planned too much material. The lesson was a bit disorganized. They found the map hard to follow and the 3D model puzzled them at first. I could have saved time by doing all the labelling at once.

Note to reader

The student made three common errors in her lesson:

1. Her objectives were too ambitious.
2. She did not clearly specify how she proposed to organize the lesson.
3. She overestimated the skills of nine-year-olds.

Notice also that her post-viewing impressions were global criticism rather than attempts to analyse and improve. Now read the lesson which she planned after completing some activities on lesson planning.

A student's second lesson planning record

Name: _V. Mitchell_   Topic area: _Journeys_   Class: _P5_   Date: _12/2/75_

Skill/s under review: _Reinforcement_   /~~Global~~   Time: _15 minutes_

Note on pupils' knowledge, if known:

1. Explicit objective/s   By the end of the lesson the pupils will be able to solve simple problems based on journeys (or 'messages') in Coleraine. They will recognize that most journeys involve crossing the bridge and — I hope — they may suggest that Coleraine needs another bridge. (Mostly cognitive)

2. Topic/method   Mostly discussion, some discovery.

   a) Introduction:

   Put up a large diagram of Coleraine. Ask children to show where they live, where the school is. Hand out diagrams on sheets.

   b) Development: Tell them they have to explain to a visitor how to get from their school to different parts of the town. Ask each pupil a simple question. I'll start with P, he's still a wee bit shy so I'll give him an easy one. (Must remember to tell them to wait their turn and not shout answers out.) Praise each pupil. Then ask more difficult questions. If answers clear, tell them so. Then give them ten questions each involving messages (shopping, clinic, park, library, swimming pool, etc. All they have to do is to tick if they cross bridge, go through the Diamond, down Queen Street.

   c) Completion: Ask them for their answers. (I'll put questions on overhead projector whilst they're doing the problems.) Ask them if they notice anything about most of the journeys (messages). Ask them which way do cars passing through the town go to get to Limavady and Londonderry. Is this a busy bridge? What could the Council do to make it less busy?

   d) Resources: Diagrams, overhead projector, pens.

   e) Pupil activities:
   Answer questions, discuss, follow map, solve problems.

3. Post-lesson impression

   Children enjoyed this. They wanted some more problems to do. Had to change question on the council to 'Should there be another bridge?' — of course they answered, Yes!

4. Post-viewing impression

   I used praise a lot and 'ah ha' too much. If anything, I over-reinforced and then couldn't get them to move on to the next part of the lesson. Must try to get the pupils to switch from one activity to another. G. suggested saying, 'That's been very interesting, let's move on now to the next bit because I think you'll find it interesting as well.' Children obviously enjoyed it. They kept opening their mouths to speak and interrupting each other, but they seem to understand the importance of taking turns. Making sure everybody got a chance to speak helped. Problem — can't see how that is possible in a large class.

Sample lesson planning records

A lesson planning record on set and closure

Name: A. Fedden   Topic area: Fire   Class: P5   Date: 20/2/75

Skill/s under review: Set and closure   ~~Global~~   Time: 15 minutes

Note on pupils' knowledge, if known: ———

1. **Explicit objective/s**

    By the end of the lesson the children will appreciate the damage fire can cause, and the importance of safety precautions. They will produce their own list of do's and dont's. (Predominantly affective attitudes.)

2. **Topic/method** — Predominantly discussion, some exposition.

    a) Introduction: — I will settle the children down, then strike a match and let it burn. Then I'll lift up the tin tray of paper houses and cotton wool. Strike another match and set the houses on fire. Then I'll say, 'Today I want to look at the damage fire can cause. Here is a photograph of some people's houses.

    b) Development: — Point to various kinds of damage in picture. (It was a fire, not a bomb.) Ask why I used a metal tray for demonstration. Ask them how fires are caused in the home. Get the children to produce a list of do's and dont's. (Always : NEVER) on the board.

    c) Completion: — Go over what they said in the lesson. Show them a fire extinguisher and how it works.

    d) Resources: — Matches, tin tray with paper houses, cotton wool damped with methylated spirit. Chalk, blackboard, jotting pads. Picture of fire damage.

    e) Pupil activities:

    look, discuss, produce list. If time, copy it down

3. **Post-lesson impression** — Children fascinated by demonstration. Wanted me to do it again. They talked a lot about fires at home. One had seen a chip pan catch fire so we talked about what to do. They produced a good list and some of them wanted to copy it down.

4. **Post-viewing impression** — The set worked very well and the next section on the picture was clearly linked to it. The pupils wanted to talk a lot about fires and their experiences. We could have spent ages on this. They were also interested in fire extinguishers. Peter said there were different kinds. I might follow this up next week.

    They watched the fire in amazement. It would have been too exciting if I had not taken some of the paper houses off before they lit. They (the pupils) wanted to talk about fire damage, but I steered them off bombs. They all had something to say this week. I think it was a success.

A lesson planning record on questioning

Name: A. Fedden   Topic area: Mollusc (common   Class: P6   Date: 20/1/75
                                            snail)

Skill/s under review: Questions and answers   ~~Global~~   Time: 15 minutes

Note on pupils' knowledge, if known: ———

1. Explicit objective/s — Hope to continue to foster interest in natural history.
   Children should be able to describe life pattern of snail. (Mostly cognitive.)

2. Topic/method — Question and answer lesson.
   a) Introduction: — Distribute illustrated cyclostyled sheet to each child. Begin
      by asking them what they can remember about molluscs from last week's
      lesson. (Recall, comprehension.) Then ask them to look at pictures of snail
      and the information on the sheet and to ask me questions.

   b) Development: — After they've asked me questions, I'll ask each of them some
      What and Why questions. (Comprehension and analysis.) e.g. What is
      hibernation? Expect answer: Going to sleep in winter. Why do some animals
      sleep, go to sleep in winter? Why do snails come out at night/dusk rather
      than in daylight? This might lead from 'so they are not eaten' to the idea
      of food chains. What do snails eat? Do snails drink? How do they get
      liquid?

   c) Completion: — Summarize what the children said in the lesson by asking
      a few questions of the whole class.

   d) Resources: — Cyclostyled sheets, snail shells, large picture of snail, chalk,
      blackboard.
   e) Pupil activities: — Looking, reading, asking questions, giving answers.

3. Post-lesson impression — Diversion. Near end of lesson children began to
   discuss the fact that french people eat snails. Some expressions of disgust,
   so I pointed out that the snails they eat are very special — and they had
   never eaten a snail so they don't know what they are like. Pointed out
   that every country has it's favourite foods and they're all different. Might
   try to do a lesson on cultural differences later.

4. Post-viewing impression —— They remembered a lot about last week's lesson
   and they liked the idea of them asking me questions. Henry asked about
   the shell of a newly-hatched snail and I used the word 'transparent'
   in my answer. Suddenly realised that they didn't understand meaning
   of this word — yet they all understood hibernation. Amazing how we
   take for granted pupils' understanding of words.

        Managed to ask everyone a question but one little boy wouldn't
   answer — he never does the first time I ask him but he will talk
   if I give him time and hints. Didn't need to use probing very much.
   I rushed some of the questions. It's very hard to pause sometimes.

A lesson planning record on participation

Name: A. Fedden   Topic area: Signs and signals   Class: P6   Date: 12/2/75

Skill/s under review: Discussion (pupil participation) ~~/Global~~   Time: 15 minutes

Note on pupils' knowledge, if known: ———

1. Explicit objective/s —— By end of lesson children will be aware that we use signs and symbols as well as speech and writing in our daily lives. This could lead to discussion of language itself. (Cognitive)

2. Topic/method —— Discussion.

   a) Introduction: —— Pupils take part in 'experiment'. They must communicate without using words. I'll ask them to pretend they are with people who do not understand English. a) HUNGRY b) THIRSTY c) TIRED d) GO AWAY.

   b) Development: —— Ask them to imagine they are in a car driving through a town. What do the road signs in the books (see Resources below) mean? What should they do when they come to the signs? Then move In   can we use to communicate? What did Red Indians use? Jungle tribes? What can ships use as well as ordinary radio?

   c) Completion: —— Recap on what we have discussed. Jot it down. Let children draw and print signs and signals to convey information. Tell them what we are going to do next week.

   d) Resources: —— Penguin project books 'Signs and Signals' (Harverson, 1972), drawing paper, jotters, fibre tip pens, chalk, blackboard.

   e) Pupil activities: —— Imagine, do code exercises, discuss, draw.

3. Post-lesson impression —— The children responded very well to lesson. They enjoyed the text books and didn't want to give them back. There was a diversion I found interesting. One of the pupils pointed out that some people are deaf and dumb and so talk with their fingers. This led to talking about blind people and braille. This gave me a chance to remind them about the lesson we had done on the senses.

4. Post-viewing impression —— Pupil participation was good. I was able to use a lot of the pupils' ideas. There was not as much discussion in the lesson as I'd expected. The introduction and code exercise took up over half the time. A (a withdrawn pupil) took part in this class, he volunteered information and drew his pictures happily. He liked the books — he can't read very well and the illustrations helped him to follow the lesson. The lesson didn't hang together as clearly as it should. If I do this topic again I'll split it up into a series of lessons.

Some pupil activities

Here is a list of ways in which pupils can be profitably active in class. Add to it out of your own experience. Occasionally consider the proportion of class time you devote to pupil activity of the kinds indicated below. Ask yourself if this is too much or too little and take the appropriate steps.

1. Completing job-card exercises.
2. Working with programmed or other auto-instructional material.
3. Systematic note-making.
4. Writing workbook exercises.
5. Summarizing the thought of a plan or passage or lesson.
6. Group discussions or debating.
7. Guided reading in response to prior questioning.
8. Completing multiple-choice, true/false or essay type questions.
9. Writing critical book reports.
10. Preparing material for class magazines or projects.
11. Carrying out experiments.
12. Demonstrating to other pupils.
13. Writing tests or answering quizzes.
14. Preparing questions on material being studied.
15. Preparing display materials for bulletin board.
16. Looking for facts.
17. Analysing data.
18. Preparing charts or models.
19. Illustrating or representing ideas pictorially.
20. Map making or completing.
21. Short practice drills.
22. Estimating answers in mathematics.
23. Making graphs from data given.
24. Translating written problems into mathematical statements.
25. Forming written problems from mathematical statements.
26. Seeking application of principles to everyday life problems.
27. Measuring.
28. Reporting.
29. Organizing facts and principles gathered from discussion, reading and stating them as clear and valid conclusions.
30. Evaluating current events.
31. Developing a map of the home community, indicating vital points of economic, political and social interest.

Concept teaching

The teaching of concepts is an important part of a teacher's repertoire. It has been chosen as an entry into component skills because it is relatively simple yet requires conceptual analysis in the planning stage and the use of skills of exposition, questioning and discussion skills. The discussion of concepts is divided into three sections: (i) What are concepts; (ii) The steps of concept teaching; (iii) Some illustrations of concept teaching. Further information on the concept teaching approach may be found in De Cecco's (1968) *Psychology of Learning and Instruction* (p. 385 *et seq.*).

What are concepts?

At the end of the first section you will be able to describe what a concept is and what attributes and attribute values are. What are concepts? Put very simply they are *classes* of stimuli which have common characteristics. Those stimuli may be objects, events or persons. Usually we attach a name or label to concepts. Examples are book, war,

Activity 8

Planned global teaching

You should now tackle the next activity. This will be your first serious attempt to plan a microteaching lesson so do it as thoroughly as you can.

Plan a ten minute lesson on any topic of your choice which may be of interest to your team of peers. Use the lesson plan provided. Teach and videorecord it. One of the team should signal to you at about the eighth minute so you can bring your lesson to a close. Assume that at the tenth minute the school bell has rung and your pupils must leave immediately for their next class. Immediately after teaching the lesson note down your impressions of the lesson. Immediately before viewing with your peers specify your objectives. View and discuss the lesson in the terms set out on the lesson plan. Complete the final section of your lesson plan.

Compare your lesson notes of Activity 2 with those of this Activity. Write a short paragraph indicating the main differences in your planning and performance in the two activities.

Keep the videorecording for use later in the course.

attractive woman, dedicated students, drugs. All concepts refer to classes of stimuli. But, of course, not all stimuli are concepts. Thus the set of stimuli you perceive and label Raquel Welch is not a concept but she is, for many men, a positive instance of the concept of attractive woman.

Concepts are not always congruent with our personal experience. They represent our attempts to clarify, control and classify our perceptions and experiences. Not all of you will agree precisely on which women are attractive nor on the attributes or characteristics of attractive woman. The concept of attractive woman is, shall we say, a 'broad one'. It can include women of various sizes, shapes and colours and it is to some extent culturally determined. Some positive instances or examples, most people would agree on. On others, there would be considerable argument.

Concept attributes

This brings us to the major difficulty in concept teaching: selecting the relevant distinguishing attribute of a concept. Let's look at the term 'student' and some examples of people categorized as students.

[44]   Suppose a student has a beard and long hair, stays in bed every morning, attends lectures only in the afternoon and spends his grant in the first three weeks of term. Now consider another student who also has long hair and a beard, but who gets up early, reads books and attends all lectures and seminars. In classifying both individuals as students, we have to ignore the non-essentials and focus upon the dominant distinguishing attributes.

If one took beards as a distinguishing attribute one would rule out most women students that I have known. If one took 'attends *all* lectures and seminars' as the distinguishing attribute we might, effectively, be saying only the lecturers are students in some universities.

What are the distinguishing attributes of the concept of 'students'? Write down a list of characteristics and decide which are the essential ones.

Attribute values

Most attributes have a wide range of values. A student may read books – from one to, say, twenty a term. The attribute of size may vary from micro to truly enormous, of weight from light to heavy and so on. A few attributes are binary, either/or. You are, for example, living or dead. There is no intermediary value.

Concepts may vary in the number of attributes. The greater the number of attributes the more complex the concept is. The attributes of a ball are few in number. There are several major attributes of a democracy and they are inextricably linked.

Finally, some attributes are more readily perceived than others and these are not necessarily the distinguishing attributes. Your task, as a concept teacher, is to draw out the major distinguishing attributes and to help children to distinguish the relevant from the irrelevant.

Concepts, then, are classes of stimuli. Examples of concepts are called positive instances. Concepts have attributes which may vary in number, in value, in perceivability and in importance. The main skills in concept teaching involve selecting appropriate concepts and examples and drawing out the major distinguishing attributes of the concepts.

The steps of concept teaching

1. Choose a concept.
   Examples : transport, tourist, solids, sport, fruit.
2. Specify explicit objectives.
   Example : By the end of this lesson the pupils will be able to outline the essential features of fruit.
3. Topics and methods.
   a. Write a list of positive instances of the concept, negative instances and any instances which are hard to decide.

Activity 9

Look at the items below and decide which letter, a, b, c, *best* distinguishes the numbered items:

1. Student
2. Several
3. Colour, size, shape
4. Two, red, enormous
5. A concept refers to a class of stimuli.

a – attributes; b – attribute values; c – concept.

See page 146 for answers

b. Identify the main important attributes and underline them. Use these in your lesson.
c. Decide whether to use predominantly lecture, discussion or guided discovery. Guided discovery is usually enjoyed by peers and pupils.
d. Plan your approach and the order in which you will tackle the attributes of the concept. Pay particular attention how you will introduce and end your lesson.
e. Introduce the concept in a familiar or acceptable context. Make sure you give the pupils opportunity and time to respond to some questions regardless of the method of presentation used.

Now re-read the section on concepts and compare it with these steps of concept teaching.

Why was such a simple definition of the concept of a concept chosen? (See page 146 for answers.)

An illustration of concept teaching

Based upon De Cecco (1968) *The Psychology of Learning and Instruction.*

1. The teacher began by saying, 'Today I want you to learn the concept "tourist". By the end of the lesson you will be able to identify quickly any examples of "tourist" I present to you.'
2. The teacher had analysed the concept 'tourist' and identified three dominant attributes, *activity, purpose* and *residence* and their particular values (travel and sightseeing, pleasure, keeping the same permanent residence). She thought of other attributes such as mode of travel, passports etc. but discarded them as minor.

3. Teacher made certain that the students had the necessary verbal associations by writing the word *tourist* and having them say it.

4. She presented positive and negative examples in the form of verbal descriptions printed on large cards, which all could see and read.

5. Each example was left in view after the presentation. Before each example she reminded the class that they were looking for a *class* of people: e.g. Mr. P. lives in Los Angeles but he is on vacation and is visiting Rome to see friends. 'Is Mr. P. a tourist?' Mr. M left India in 1940 and has raised his children in England where he now lives. 'Is Mr. M a tourist?'

6. The teacher presented a new positive example of the concept 'tourist', e.g. Mr. A, who had lived in X for 30 years, was returning to his native land to sightsee. Is he a tourist?

7. She then presented several new positive and negative examples of individuals who were both tourists and immigrants at different times.

8. The teacher asked pupils to write a definition of a tourist, asking them to keep in mind how a tourist is different from an immigrant.

9. Finally she reminded them of the original objectives and gave a test in which she included both positive and negative examples.

Note: The steps beyond 6 were not designed for original concept learning but were the means of verifying, preserving and extending the learning which had occurred.

In teaching concepts you can decide to stop at step 6 or continue, as time and purpose suggest.

Activity 10

Peer teaching

Choose a concept from the school curriculum which you think is relevant to the age range of pupils you will be teaching during the microteaching course. Plan and teach a concept lesson to your peers. View and discuss it. Complete the lesson record.

Activity 11

Pupil teaching

In this activity you are asked to teach a small group of pupils. Before the lessons begins you should get to know the children, which school they are from and whether this is their first visit to the microteaching laboratories. If it is, you should point out the cameras and, if there is time, you or the person coordinating microteaching should promise to let the group see an extract from the videotapes. The children may be excited at this prospect so do not tell them this until *after* you have taught them. Pupils rapidly adjust to the microteaching set-up but during their first lesson they may play up to the cameras. In subsequent lessons such behaviour is usually a sign of boredom. Later on in the programme you might like to show them further extracts from lessons and perhaps discuss them. If you do, be prepared for frank views.

Your task in Activity 11

Teach the modified lesson based on Activity 10. View and discuss it. Complete the lesson record.

The videorecording of this lesson should be retained until the end of the programme.

Summary of units on planning

Units I and II have introduced you to lesson planning and concept teaching. Lesson planning in microteaching consists of selecting a topic, writing explicit objectives and developing an appropriate order of subtopics in relation to the teaching methods chosen. These methods may be expositions, discussions or guided discoveries. Each have their advantages and disadvantages. The lesson planning record includes a description of the plan and a summary of post-lesson impressions and discussion. A description of 'hidden objectives' and digressions are an important part of the summary. Concepts in their simplest form are sets of stimuli with common attributes. Concept teaching consists of generating positive, negative and borderline instances and identifying the important attributes. The concept teaching lesson is built around the essential attributes of the concept. Throughout the remainder of the teaching skills programme you will be using the lesson record and you will find various disguised examples of concept teaching in subsequent units.

You should now re-read the first paragraph of Unit I (p. 21) and Activity 2. Your perception of their meaning should have been changed through the experience of working through the units. The next units consider ways of perceiving teaching. Their meaning and value will become evident as you gain in experience and expertise in microteaching.

Suggestions for further reading

For a systematic view of the vast field covered in these units you should read:

DE CECCO, J. P. (1968) *The Psychology of Learning and Instruction,* Prentice-Hall.
KLAUSMEIER, H. J. and RIPPLE, R. E. (1971) *Learning and Human Abilities,* 3rd edition, Harper & Row.

The associated readings contain reprints of several scholarly studies:

DE CECCO, J. (1967) *Psychology of Language, Thought and Instruction: Readings,* Holt Rinehart & Winston.
RIPPLE, R. E. (1971) *Readings in Learning and Human Abilities,* 2nd edition, Harper & Row.
STONES, E. (1970) *Readings in Educational Psychology: Learning and Teaching,* Methuen.

For a comprehensive guide on teaching you should consult:

PETERSON, A. D. C. (1966) *The Techniques of Teaching,* Vol. 1 *Primary,* Vol. 2 *Secondary,* Pergamon Press.

The following texts on specific topics may be helpful. On instructional objective writing:

MAGER, R. F. (1962) *Preparing Instructional Objectives,* Fearon Press, Palo Alto, California.
POPHAM, W. J. *et al.* (1969) *Instructional Objectives,* Rand McNally.

On topic and task analyses (this is a difficult field):

DAVIES, I. F. (1971) *The Organization of Learning,* McGraw-Hill.
STONES, E. and ANDERSON, D. (1972) *Educational Objectives and the Teaching of Educational Psychology,* Methuen.

For a description of discovery learning:

FOSTER, J. (1972) *Discovery Learning in the Primary School,* Routledge & Kegan Paul.

On teaching methods designed to promote imaginative problem solving in secondary school children:

DAVID, G. A. and HOUTMAN, S. E. (1968) *Thinking Creatively: A Guide to Training Imagination,* Wisconsin Research and Development Centre for Cognitive Learning.
DE BONO, E. (1973) *CoRT Thinking,* Direct Education Services, Blandford Forum.

On item and question writing, and measuring pupil performance:

HUDSON, B. (ed) (1973) *Assessment Techniques: An Introduction,* Methuen.
SANDERS, N. (1966) *Classroom Questions: What kinds,* Harper & Row.

Unit III · Perceiving teaching

Section One contained a brief description of the marked variations in the perceptions of teaching. Subjectivity is likely to be at its highest when viewing one's own performance. It is also likely to be most intrusive when you have no clear guide lines of what to look for. Salomon and McDonald (1970) in an interesting experiment compared students' unstructured responses to viewing themselves on videotape after microteaching. About 18 per cent of the free responses were concerned with teaching behaviour, the remainder was largely a mixture of derisory comments about themselves or the subjects they were teaching. If you are to benefit from video or audiotape feedback and from observing others teach or learn then some training in ways of observing is necessary. This unit and the following one have been written with this in mind. They have three objectives. First, to introduce you to ways of looking into teaching as well as at it. Secondly, to train you in the use of various approaches and thirdly, to give you some help in the interpretation of the data you may collect from the analyses of your lessons. On reading the units carefully and assiduously carrying out the activities you will sharpen your perceptual skills and will be able to identify and discuss a variety of observation techniques. You may also be in a position to compare what you planned to do in your lessons with your actual performance.

On perception and teaching

What we see is determined partly by our linguistic competencies, expectancies, attitudes and values stored in our central processes. Figure 6 gives two examples.

Figure 6a. Read the words in the figure. *Figure 6b.* What's this?

PARIS IN THE

THE SPRING

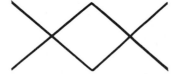

Now read them slowly. Describe in words.

Figure 6a is a commonplace illustration. Most people first read it as 'Paris in the spring'. We expect a noun after the definite article not another definite article. We therefore see it that way. Figure 6b evokes different descriptions: two crosses, two V's and their reflection, a W and its reflection, a diamond with whiskers, part of a trellis, part of a pair of sugar tongs, a geometrical problem or a freemasonry sign. Each set of verbal descriptions shapes what you see. The only one which might cause you difficulty is the freemasonry sign – if you know little about freemasonry.

If what we see in a set of monosyllables and a line diagram is determined by what is stored in our heads then it is at least arguable that what we see in teaching is also powerfully shaped by our central processes. As we gain knowledge – be it freemasonry or the business of teaching – so what we see changes in meaning and significance. Activity 2 had a different meaning to you after you had read the whole section on planning. The string of numbers 10 10 10 10 7 7 7 9 9 9 7 7 7 7 6 7 10 10 10 means little to you at present. On completing the next unit it will have a significance.

P-type and A-type methods of observing

Techniques of observing and evaluating teaching may be placed upon a continuum ranging from the relatively open, unstructured and unsystematic to the closed, highly structured and systematic. The two poles may be described as the phenomenological and the analytic approach. Figure 7 sets out the main features.

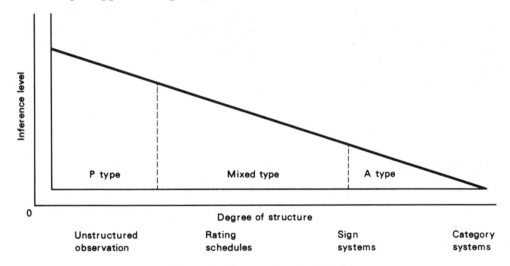

Figure 7. Observational methods

Inference level refers to the complexity of the variables observed and reported. High inference variables contain several inter-related elements, low inference variables contain fewer. Warmth is a high inference variable, smiling is a low inference variable. High inference variables may be observed and rated, low inference variables may also be counted. Structure, at its minimum, is global and relatively undifferentiated. As one moves along the axis, structure becomes more precise and differentiated. Birdwhistell's (1970) analysis of over one hundred facial movements is an extreme example of precision. Agreement between observers is least likely to occur at extreme points of the observation model. Global subjective descriptions and very precise, extensive category systems should therefore be avoided for feedback and evaluation puposes.

Phenomenological or P-type methods are the most commonly used and misused. Whenever an observer sits at the back of a class and writes continuous notes on the happenings he is using P-type methods. His report may include high or low inference variables. P-type methods shade off into rating schedules which ostensibly have more structure but are usually concerned with high inference variables. These gradually merge into A-type methods. These are sign and category systems, they are highly structured and they usually focus upon low inference variables.

All observation methods may be carried out on live or recorded data. The record may be audio-visual, visual, audio or tapescripts (tapescripts are transcripts of tape recordings). Information loss is highest in tapescripts but this is offset by the opportunities to closely analyse linguistic features of teaching (Bellack and Davitz, 1963). All observation methods involve selective perception which excludes as well as includes information. P-type methods have no ground rules except 'look and see'. A-type methods require the acquisition of the rules of the system. P-type methods are defiantly value-laden whereas values operate in A-type methods in the choice of category systems and the interpretation of results. Moving from P- to A-type methods does not eliminate subjectivity but it does control it and change the level at which it operates. It is worth noting that all methods involve some inference and some structure. There is no escape into the womb of positivism or the clouds of mysticism. The remainder of this unit contains examples, activities and discussions of various methods of observing teaching. We begin with a few examples from P-type reports by Roy Nash (1973) who spent over a year observing in Scottish classrooms and writing on what he saw.

Examples of P-type reports

1. FROM A SPELLING LESSON

The class all spelt out 'apparatus' in chorus. A bit ragged. 'Give me some examples of apparatus'. A boy calls out, 'Kidney machine'. Teacher looks at him. Not very friendly, I think. The boy repeats his answer. Teacher looks at him again and appears to consider it. 'No, that's an instrument.' Class looks stunned. 'Oh, come on. There's lots of things.' (School E)

(Nash, 1973, pp. 53–54)

2. FROM A DISCUSSION LESSON

The pupils were being asked to choose a topic for a debate. The pupils made suggestions and the teacher wrote some of them down. One suggestion was 'Children should not get the belt'.

'Oh, how many of you think that children shouldn't get the belt?' Almost all hands go up. 'Well, it looks like you've out-voted yourselves, if you all agree there won't be any debate. I've a feeling that I'm going to veto this one. What does veto mean?' 'Bung it out.' 'Get rid of it.' Several children reply. 'Um, yes. I don't mind but some people . . . now sensible ones.' A girl suggests debating whether they should have a shorter dinner hour and leave school earlier in the afternoon. Teacher likes this suggestion and erases the question about belting and adds this to the list. A few more suggestions come up – going to the moon, capital punishment – a boy suggests, 'Children should be allowed to eat in class.' Lots of calls for this. 'Yes, yes.' 'Oh no,' says the teacher, 'that's silly, we're not having that.' The children are a bit excited at this prospect of having some discussion about their lives in school. 'Children should not be allowed to be teachers' pets' is suggested. There is overwhelming response to this. Lots of enthusiastic agreement. 'Oh, no. Now you are being silly. We're not doing that. Now I want some sensible ones or we'll go back to arithmetic.'

(Nash, 1973, p. 55)

3. OBSERVATION RECORD: ROBERT

Most of the class are doing project work. Three boys still seem to be doing English. This means they haven't finished quickly enough. Teacher looks over to them. 'Robert, you could be doing an excellent drawing for me but you're so slow with your English.' Robert looks glum. He puts down his pencil. Looks like he's finished at last – or given up. He goes to the teacher who is telling Albert what a 'lovely wee campfire' he has painted. She sees Robert standing a bit behind her not drawing attention to himself. 'Ah, now you can help me here,' she says. She heads him over to the model tray. 'We're going to have the Rockies either side and that's going to be a wee pass. Are you very good at making mountain shapes?' Robert looks doubtfully at the heap of papiermâché. 'No?' asks the teacher. 'Well, I'll get someone else to do that then.' She tells him to do a picture instead. Robert goes back to his desk. He looks about, sees that he hasn't any paper to draw on and decides to finish his English. A couple of minutes later teacher asks the class, 'Anyone still doing English?' Robert raises his hand. 'Oh come on, Robert,' she says.

(Nash, 1973, p. 33)

Activity 12

a. Identify a low and a high inference variable in each of examples 1 and 2.
b. Write a paragraph describing your perceptions of the teacher's behaviour and attitude in each of the examples given. Substantiate your views with reference to the phenomenological data. Compare your views with those of other members of your teaching team.

The answers to part a. are given at the end of the book (p. 146).

Discussion of Activity 12

The examples are very brief so one's descriptions are at best tentative. Example 1 suggests that the teacher probably did not like the boy's response or perhaps even the boy himself. The teacher may have been looking for specific answers which did not include 'kidney machine'. There are many instances of such behaviours in classrooms. The question appears open but only specific answers are actually wanted by the teacher. Barnes (1969)

refers to them as pseudo-questions. Stuart (1969) describes pupils' answers that conform [53]
to teacher expectations as 'crawl' answers. Pseudo-questions and 'crawl' answers are
value-laden terms. They may have their place in teaching. The point is to be aware
of them and decide upon their appropriateness.

Example 2 shows a teacher steering off a sensitive area of pupil life and the teacher's
role. It ends with a threat that makes most mathematicians wince. Example 3 shows
a teacher mildly reprimanding a boy, dangling an enjoyable activity, removing it and
the boy retreating back to his task only to be reproved again. One might deduce that
the teacher treats Robert as 'not very able' and lacking in confidence. Her treatment
is in line with her perceptions. She described Robert in an interview with Nash as
tending to be lazy, emotionally disturbed, lacking confidence, shy and of low IQ. How
far our perceptions of children govern their behaviour with us is a question worth
contemplating.

Your phenomenological reports may not contain any of the above points. There are
no right or wrong answers in this game. Through discussing specific examples of teaching
you become aware of meanings and structures. Let us now turn to a P-type analysis
of some tapescripts. Until the advent of multi-media packages, this is the nearest one
can get to the live situation. Seeing the words on the page actually has some advantages
as you will shortly discover

Activity 13

A student teacher, Lyndsay, was asked to teach a lesson involving pupil
participation. She had seen a social skills demonstration of the skills
involved. She had been advised to choose a topic which would interest
her pupils (aged 11–12), and to think out carefully an interesting way
of introducing the topic. She was a highly intelligent graduate and she
had been a pupil at a girls' public school of high repute. This was her
first experience of microteaching. The classes were in each case nine
pupils from the top stream of a local grammar school. Read the
tapescripts through twice. On the second reading look for links between
this paragraph of background information and the lessons and viewing
session. Jot down your impressions of the lessons and the viewing
session as you read them. Look through your jottings and prepare a
paragraph on each of the lessons and the viewing session.

Lesson One (Sample from tapescript)

Lyndsay pushes door open sharply, enters, slams door, marches over to desk and without looking at the pupils she says, 'O.K., we want to read this through quite quickly and then we'll translate.' She opens book decisively and reads from it without looking at children.

TEACHER. 'The Silent Masters.' The saucer descended quickly. Down it came, closer and closer to the ground, until it was descending at great speed. Within ten feet of the ground it seemed to top and hiss and then descend again more slowly until without a sound it touched the earth for the first time. Tolman would be delighted at such a successful landing. A reconnaissance party stepped from the saucer and looked around. Periodically a cracking sound reached their hidden ears. Facing their radar antennae towards it they advanced. Soon they came within sight of a particularly green field. On this were a number of the species labelled Drevna by their telescopic machines. They were completely white and performing some strange ceremony. The Letto men knew these Drevna to be completely inferior on the earth. The Selmas were the master race. They went round to the back of the oval where the ceremony was taking place, and searched for the Selmas who were always to be found near a group of Drevna. The Tolmans had been told that the Selmas were smaller than the Drevna and walked in a peculiar manner, sometimes with Drevna. Soon the Tolmans found one of the Selmas. They carried it off whilst none of the Drevna was looking and returned to the saucer to interrogate it. It would not speak. 'Strongwilled', thought the Tolmans. There came a sudden scream from the Drevna at the ceremony. Quickly the Tolmans started up the fire chambers to the saucer before the other Drevna had seen it. There was a hiss as it left the ground and then it floated skywards. After making a brilliant century the village postman was clean bowled. One old man in the crowd did not cheer, but muttered something about having lost his dog.

TEACHER (*Firmly closes book, folds her arms, looks at the class quickly.*) Right, were there any words you didn't understand in that? Apart from the proper names because those were quite difficult. (*Pupil puts up hand.*) Yes?

PUPIL Interrogate.

TEACHER (*Stares at pupil.*) Interrogate – that means to ask or question. They were going to take him back to ask him some questions about himself. Anything else? (*Short pause.*) O.K. Can anyone tell me what they think this might be about? (*Pause.*) Yes?

PUPIL A spaceship landing on the earth.

TEACHER On the earth. Anybody else? (*Short pause.*) Did you all think that? Now, can you tell me what a Drevna might be? (*Pause.*)

PUPIL The head of the ship.

TEACHER The head of the . . .? What does anyone else think?

PUPIL The head of the people that saw it.

TEACHER The Drevna? (*Pause.*) Look again at your work. (*Long pause.*)

PUPIL A special kind of people.

TEACHER A special kind of people who live on . . .?

PUPIL On this planet.

TEACHER What is the planet this sort of men live on?

PUPIL Earth.

TEACHER Well, what are the Drevna?

PUPIL Us.

TEACHER Us, of course. Now the Selmas. They were the other people who were found on the earth when the saucer landed. What do you think they might have been? They were considered the superior race on earth. (*Pause.*)

PUPIL The ladies and lords.

TEACHER The ladies and lords. What does anyone else think? (*Pause.*) Well, look again at
    that piece of reading. 'They went round to the back of the oval where the ceremony was
    taking place, and searched for the Selmas who were always to be found near a group
    of the Drevna. The Tolman had been told that the Selmas were smaller than the Drevna
    and walked in a peculiar manner, sometimes with Drevna. (*Pause.*)
PUPIL An animal.
TEACHER Yes, what sort of an animal?
PUPIL A dog.
TEACHER A dog, that's right. O.K., now who do you think Tolman might be?
PUPIL He might be a king on a spaceship from a different planet.
TEACHER From a different planet?
PUPIL Yes.
TEACHER And he might be what?
PUPIL The leader.
TEACHER Yes, the leader of these Tolmans who are the people who came in this flying saucer
    to visit earth. Do you think there is any sort of meaning in this piece? (*Pause.*) We called
    it the Silent Masters, and you see how the saucer came to earth and found people called
    the Drevna, what they called the Drevna, and also an animal called Selmas who they
    thought superior to the Drevna. Do you think there is any sort of meaning in this? (*Pause.*)
    Do any of you have animals at home? Kate, you have.
PUPIL Horses.
TEACHER Horses? Do you keep many?
PUPIL Six.
TEACHER Six horses. Anybody else keep horses? Jenny, you keep dogs. Well, it's about dogs
    in this, isn't it? And they call the dogs the silent masters. Do you think it possible that
    dogs could master human beings?
PUPIL Yes.
TEACHER In what ways?
PUPIL A big dog could kill a man.
TEACHER Yes, that's true. Any other things? What sort of things do you do with an animal
    that you keep in the house – a pet?
PUPIL You wash and feed it and take it for a walk at night.
TEACHER That's right. You pay court to the animal, don't you? Isn't that right? O.K. How
    would you describe this sort of writing? Is it a real life sort of thing, or what?
PUPIL It's sort of imaginary.
TEACHER Imaginary? It is imaginary, isn't it? It's what we call a fantasy. Now we can all
    enter into a world of fantasy, but how can we do that? You probably do it quite a lot – I
    know I do.
PUPIL Daydream.
TEACHER Yeah, and what?
PUPIL Some people close their eyes.
TEACHER Yeah, and what do you do when you close your eyes?
PUPIL Dream.
TEACHER Yeah, but during the day, what do you call it?
PUPIL Daydreaming.
TEACHER Daydreaming. And what do most of you think about when you're daydreaming?
    Do you think about one thing in particular or many things?
PUPIL Different sorts of things.
TEACHER Different sorts of things. What about you? Different sorts of things? Well, let's think
    about what sorts of things you dream about. We'll put them on the board and see if all

the class dream about the same things. (*Pause.*) Do you think about what you're going to do when you leave school? (*Pause.*) What do you think about when you're daydreaming? (*Pause.*)

PUPIL Christmas.

TEACHER Christmas. Does anybody else think about Christmas?

(End of sample of tapescript)

The viewing session

Lyndsay, the other three members of the teaching team and the supervisor met to view and discuss the lesson. The tapescript reads.

SUPERVISOR Well, Lyndsay, tell us first (*takes pipe from mouth*) what you were trying to do in the lesson.

LYNDSAY I don't think it was particularly good. (*Looks at supervisor.*)

SUPERVISOR Mm Mm.

LYNDSAY I was trying to get them to talk about their fantasies

SUPERVISOR Is that why you chose the scientific fiction passage?

LYNDSAY (*Hesitatingly.*) Well, er, yes. I think it was rather a difficult passage.

SUPERVISOR Well, let's have a look at the tape. (*Supervisor switches on tape. One of the students lights a cigarette. Supervisor lights pipe. They sit watching the whole lesson. Supervisor switches tape off.*)

SUPERVISOR (*Turning to Lyndsay.*) Well, what do you think of it?

LYNDSAY Oh, my God. It's absolutely ghastly. (*Rest of group laughs nervously.*)

SUPERVISOR Well it wasn't as bad as all that. It was your first try.

LYNDSAY You're just being nice. It was horrible. I didn't look at any of the pupils. I went too quickly. I didn't get them talking.

SUPERVISOR (*Interrupting.*) What about the pupils?

LYNDSAY What about them?

SUPERVISOR What do you think they thought?

LYNDSAY Mmm. I don't know. (*Pause.*) They tried hard but it was too difficult for them. They didn't see what I was getting at.

SUPERVISOR Don't you think you were trying to do too much?

LYNDSAY (*Disconsolately.*) I suppose so.

SUPERVISOR What do you think, James?

JAMES (*Coughs nervously.*) Er mm er. I don't know. Maybe it was a bit too much like a standard English lesson, the sort we did at school where you could easily get caught out. That probably bothered the kids.

SUPERVISOR Rosalyn?

ROSALYN I think (*looking at Lyndsay*) you were nervous and so you came over a wee bit brisk, hard sort of. But you did get them talking a bit towards the end.

SUPERVISOR Yes, er, I think that's right. You were nervous so you clammed up but gradually you relaxed and it got better. Your questions and hints were good but I think you probably clammed up yesterday when you were preparing your lesson. Is that right?

LYNDSAY Yes. I just did not know what to do. It seemed easy when you did it but when I got here I just couldn't think of anything to do and spent all my time thinking about that, not how to do it.

SUPERVISOR I agree. It is difficult and you did what we all do when we meet a difficulty. You retreated to something you knew and had seen – a comprehension lesson. Let's see if between you, you can think of another topic. No, wait a minute. Let's look at the rest of the tapes first and then come back to this. Incidentally, Lyndsay, it wasn't half as bad as you thought. A different topic will work wonders.

LYNDSAY Mmm . . .

Lesson Two

After the viewing session Lyndsay prepared another lesson on the skills of pupil participation. She had another class of nine pupils from the top stream of the first year of a local grammar school. The tapescript reads:

Lyndsay enters room, stops at door. Looks and smiles at the class and without saying anything hands to each pupil a sheet of paper. She walks to the board, turns and smiles.

TEACHER (*In a soft, gentle voice.*) Have any of you ever been to a foreign country? (*Pause.*) You have? Where have you been?

PUPIL England.

TEACHER (*Looks at pupil in a friendly way.*) England. Did you like it there? Which part did you go to?

PUPIL London.

TEACHER London. So you went to Buckingham Palace and the Tower . . . (*Pupil shakes head to say, no.*) No? None of those places? (*Pause.*) Was it a long time ago?

PUPIL Yes. We sent to stay with my auntie.

TEACHER That must have been nice. (*Pause.*) Anybody else been somewhere?

PUPIL Africa.

TEACHER (*Opens eyes wide.*) Africa. Which part?

PUPIL Nigeria.

TEACHER Oh! I bet that was nice. What sort of things did you see there?

PUPIL We went to the University and we went to villages and one day we went into the bush.

TEACHER Did you like that?

PUPIL Yes. My daddy worked there – that's why we were there.

TEACHER Oh, I see. What were the people like?

PUPIL They were very friendly.

TEACHER Were they? Of course, it's a lot hotter there, isn't it? Anybody else been somewhere? (*Pause.*) No. You've all stayed in Ireland. (*Smiles.*) Well, that's something nice you've got to do later, then. Now, (*Pause.*) have any of you ever had strange children come to this school? Visitors, I mean, from another country.

PUPIL No.

TEACHER Well, if someone came to see you, where would you take him?

PUPIL The safari park.

TEACHER That's near the Causeway. What sort of things do you have there?

PUPIL Lions.

TEACHER Just lions? Are they all sort of prowling around? It's not like a zoo – they're not in cages, are they?

PUPIL No.

TEACHER How do you (*gestures with hands*) sort of protect yourselves?

PUPIL Stay in the car. You can't get out of the car, you just drive around.

TEACHER Do you go quite slowly in the bus? – so you don't scare the animals? (*Pause.*) I suppose that's nice. Is it open all the year round? (*Pause.*) So that's a good one all year. Now, anything else? (*Writes on blackboard.*)

PUPIL Giant's Causeway.

TEACHER (*Opens eyes wide.*) Now what's particularly interesting about that?

PUPIL There's the rocks.

TEACHER Rocks (*Nods head*).

PUPIL 'Wishing Chair.'

TEACHER 'Wishing Chair.' Is that a sort of rock formation?

PUPIL Yes. (*Transcript obscure.*)

TEACHER Oh, you can wish on it? Do you know what other sort of rock formations are there? (*Writes on blackboard.*)

PUPIL It's called a hexagon.

TEACHER Does anyone know what shape a hexagon is? How many sides has it got?

PUPIL Six.

TEACHER Is it six? It might be six, actually. One, two, three, four, five, six. Yes, six. There we are: we've both learnt something. Now. Well, that's the Giant's Causeway. Now, isn't there something quite near the Giant's Causeway which isn't part of it, but you can go along to it from the Giant's Causeway?

PUPIL Dunluce Castle.

TEACHER Dunluce Castle. Would that be a good place to take children? Do any of you know when that was built? (*Writes on blackboard.*)

PUPIL When the Vikings came.

TEACHER The Vikings?

PUPIL Yes.

TEACHER So it's been here since about . . . When did the Vikings come? Any of you know?

PUPIL 1066?

TEACHER Not quite. About the . . . What century? About the seventh century (so that's quite a good place to take him). What sort of state is it in now? Is it fairly upright?

PUPIL Derelict.

TEACHER Derelict, is it?

PUPIL Well, some of the kitchen has fallen away.

TEACHER The kitchen? Now, that's the one that's right on the edge of the cliff, isn't it? Do you need some sort of admission money for it?

PUPIL Yes.

TEACHER How much?

PUPIL Two shillings, I think.

TEACHER That's quite a lot. It's, what now? – two shillings – ten pence. Now, is there a castle in Coleraine? (*Pause.*) No? Not in Coleraine, but there is one further along.

PUPIL Oh, Downhill Castle.

TEACHER Downhill Castle. That's right. (*Smiles.*) Do any of you know this?

PUPIL Yes.

TEACHER Do you live near it? Is it better than this castle?

PUPIL It's better built.

TEACHER . . . and it's more upright. There's more remaining, is there? I imagine it hasn't been there so long. That's Downhill. Who lived there? Anybody know who lived there? (*Writes on blackboard.*)

PUPIL Irish kings . . . Romans

TEACHER Well, actually it wasn't really a castle. It was built to look like a castle. It's the Bishop of Londonderry . . . used to have donkey rides along the beach. Now there's something else in the grounds of Downhill palace which I think is interesting, because I've seen it on my way to Coleraine every day.

PUPIL Is it a tower?

TEACHER It is. It's a sort of tower.

PUPIL Wall?

TEACHER No. (*Shakes head gently.*) It does have walls.

PUPIL Oh, it's a temple.

TEACHER Temple. The Mussenden Temple, That's right. That would be quite a good place to go, I should say.

PUPIL Please miss, there are tombstones in the Temple.

TEACHER Are there? I've never been inside – I don't know.

PUPIL There's a railway down underneath Mussenden Temple.

TEACHER That's right. That's the railway I come on from Londonderry.

(End of sample of tapescript)

Discussion of the tapescripts

Lyndsay's first lesson was not untypical of many first attempts at teaching. Despite her intellectual and literary gifts she retreated to the kind of English teaching she may have experienced many times as a pupil. She distanced herself socially from the class, she used silence and a stare in response to the first pupil answer and so discouraged pupil participation. She chose a passage which required high level thinking and she did not give the pupils time to mull over it. It was rather like asking you to comment on an oral presentation of the tapescripts instead of a written one. She did give prompts, and probed the children's answers which is praiseworthy particularly in a beginner.

These points were covered in the viewing session. The supervisor did not rattle them off. Lyndsay herself made most of them and the supervisor and the other members of the team commented and supported her. Students, I should add, initially dislike commenting upon each other's lessons. The supervisor did not flood Lyndsay with information and comment. He ended the session with the suggestion that only the choice of topic was wrong and that all would be well next time. 'A different topic will work wonders . . .'

It did, as you see in the second lesson. She chose a topic of interest, presented the children with a problem to discuss. She established a friendly relationship, began her lesson with a simple question, and she used smiles, interested looks and praise. She incorporated the pupils' ideas into her discussion and she wrote the main points on the board. At the risk of punning, the change in her teaching was phenomenal.

Activity 14

Plan and teach a lesson in which you try to gain pupil participation.
During the viewing session write down a continuous record of what
you observe. Give yourself and your fellow teachers a mark out of 15
for the lessons. In the discussion that follows the viewing compare your
P-type reports on the lessons and the marks awarded.

From global ratings to rating schedules

You have just used the oldest, easiest and most useless method of evaluating teaching: the global rating. Your P-type reports and marks of each other's teaching may all be different. You may have awarded the same mark for different reasons or a different mark for the same reasons. When used in classrooms the global rating is a crude measure indeed. For it is used to compare the performance of teachers working with different age and ability groups of pupils, teaching different subjects and different types of lessons. The global rating itself is singularly uninformative. It does not itself indicate the criteria or tell a student how he can improve his teaching.

Because global ratings are so unhelpful there has been a movement away from them and towards the use of rating schedules. A simple example of a rating schedule is given below. It is based upon Ryan's (1960) detailed study of the characteristics of 6,000 teachers. Factor analysis yielded these three separate broad dimensions of teaching behaviours.

X_0 Warm, friendly v cold, hostile, aloof
        7 6 5   4   3 2 1

Y_0 Systematic, businesslike v disorganized, unsystematic, slipshod
            7 6 5   4   3 2 1

Z_0 Stimulating, imaginative, v dull, boring, unimaginative
    enthusiastic   7 6 5   4   3 2 1

The X_0, Y_0, Z_0, scales are useful for a quick assessment of teaching – particularly when the observer looks and listens to teachers and pupils. They are nonetheless high inference variables and so do not help a student to improve his teaching. The injunction 'Be warmer' may have little meaning to a beginner. On the other hand, Ryan's scales were based on well over two hundred original items and this amount of information might prove overwhelming. If one is to use a rating schedule in a training programme it should contain only a small number of items and it should be based upon the component skills under review or upon a composite of the component skills of the programme. On the next page you will find a seven item scale developed for microteaching and known as the Classroom Guidance Schedule. Each item is related to at least one component skill of the programme.

CLASSROOM GUIDANCE SCHEDULE

Student: Class:

School: Topic:

Date: Observer/Teacher:

Observe the student-teacher and pupils carefully during the lesson
and then complete the Classroom Guidance Schedule. Assess the
student on each separate item as if he was about to qualify as a
teacher. In cases of doubt always give the extreme ratings (1 and 2;
6 and 7) rather than those in the middle of the scale. Put a ring
round the number which most closely indicates your view of the
student-teacher's performance. 1 is a low score and 7 a high score.
Write a brief constructive comment on each item.

1.   Skill in gaining attention (Set) | 1 | 2 | 3 | 4 | 5 | 6 | 7 |

2.   Skill in explaining, describing, narrating,
     and giving directions (Presentation) | 1 | 2 | 3 | 4 | 5 | 6 | 7 |

3.   Skill in asking and adapting questions to
     pupils (Effective questioning) | 1 | 2 | 3 | 4 | 5 | 6 | 7 |

4.   Skill in recognizing pupils' difficulties
     of understanding (Listening) | 1 | 2 | 3 | 4 | 5 | 6 | 7 |

5.   Skill in encouraging appropriate pupil
     responses (Pupil reinforcement and
     participation) | 1 | 2 | 3 | 4 | 5 | 6 | 7 |

6.   Use of non-verbal cues, e.g. gestures and
     facial expressions (Teacher liveliness) | 1 | 2 | 3 | 4 | 5 | 6 | 7 |

7.   Lesson planning and structure - as
     performed by the student-teacher (Lesson | 1 | 2 | 3 | 4 | 5 | 6 | 7 |
     planning)

Comments:

Please retain in lesson folder. This is a feedback form.

Verbal description of CGS ratings
(for observing one's own teaching)

1. Skill in gaining attention
7 indicates you very effectively gained attention
   at the beginning of the teaching episodes.
4 indicates your attempts to gain attention were
   barely successful.
1 indicates you did not gain attention at the
   beginning of a teaching episode.

*2. Skill in explaining, describing, narrating or giving
directions*
7 indicates you were consistently clear, coherent
   and understood by all the pupils.
4 indicates you were, on the whole, fairly clear
   and coherent and understood by most of the
   pupils.
1 indicates you confused your pupils.

3. Skill in asking and adapting questions
7 indicates your questions were consistently clear
   and coherent, and were well distributed and you
   used follow up questions effectively.
4 indicates your questions were on the whole
   fairly clear and coherent and you attempted to
   distribute your questions and use follow-up
   questions effectively.
1 indicates your questions were predominantly
   confusing and your follow-up questions were
   unhelpful.

*4. Skill in recognizing pupils' difficulties of
understanding*
7 indicates you quickly recognized and responded
   to pupils' difficulties of understanding.

4 indicates you recognized and responded to some
   of the difficulties of understanding.
1 indicates you failed to recognize pupils'
   difficulties of understanding.

5. Skill in encouraging appropriate pupil responses
7 indicates you effectively used a wide range of
   non-verbal, extra-verbal and verbal cues to
   develop and control pupil responses.
4 indicates you used a range of non-verbal,
   extra-verbal and verbal cues to develop and
   control pupil responses – but you were only
   marginally effective.
1 indicates you ineffectively used non-verbal,
   extra-verbal and verbal cues to develop and
   control pupil responses.

6. Use of non-verbal cues
7 indicates you most successfully used a wide
   range of non-verbal cues (smiling, facial
   expressions, gestures, movements) to convey
   warmth and meaning.
4 indicates you used a wide range of non-verbal
   cues to convey warmth and meaning.
1 indicates you were expressionless and almost
   wooden.

7. Lesson planning (as performed in the lesson)
7 indicates your teaching was highly organized
   and systematic.
4 indicates your teaching was organized and quite
   sytematic.
1 indicates your teaching was disorganized and no
   planning was detectable.

The Classroom Guidance Schedule was based upon a 14-item scale known as the Lesson Appraisal Guide (See Appendix A). Both emphasize the use of non-verbal as well as verbal communication. Some recent research indicates that the Lesson Appraisal Guide (and presumably therefore the Classroom Guidance Schedule) favours students who score high on measures of enthusiasm, sociability and logical structure (Spelman, 1974). Like all rating schedules, the Classroom Guidance Schedule makes public the values of its constructor. This is perhaps the central importance of rating schedules. They reveal to students and others the values which are operating in the training system. Debate about the nature of good teaching is made more rational. The items direct your attention to the salient features of performance and so they may be also regarded as performance objectives.

Some of my colleagues persuasively argue that the items are valuable training pointers but that the actual ratings from 1 to 7 are not. They point out that they want to encourage students to learn and so are reluctant to use the lower end of the scale. Some nine-year-old pupils appear to agree with this. When asked why they had rated a new group of microteaching students so highly one of them replied, 'Well, sir, you see they're just beginning so we thought we ought to be kind to them.' Another perceptively remarked, 'It must be a hard job, teaching us lot.' Other colleagues have pointed out that it seems unfair to assess someone at the beginning of microteaching in a way they would assess a student on his final teaching practice or in his first year in school. Students' self ratings are also likely to change as they gain in experience of teaching and observing teaching. Their perceptions of teaching as well as their performance changes during a microteaching programme, particularly when they are using the A-type methods described in the next unit.

All these points have some validity. One must ask what the rating is being used for. If it is to assess changes in performance then one needs to set a uniform standard and train raters to use it. Hence the phrase 'as if you were about to qualify as a teacher' on the Classroom Guidance Schedule which is used in the early and later stages of this training programme. If it is to encourage students to improve then the precision of the ratings does not matter. All the rating guides in this programme have been used by supervisors and students at the New University of Ulster. (Estimates of their reliability and validity were obtained and are reported in Brown, 1973.)

The Classroom Guidance Schedule uses relatively high inference and low structured variables. On page 64 are some items from two other rating schedules used in this programme. Look at them carefully and work out how they differ from the Classroom Guidance Schedule.

The Pupil Reinforcement Guide contains low inference variables which are relatively well-defined and countable. Users are asked to estimate the frequency of occurrence of the behaviours. The schedule is therefore nearer to an A-type observation than a P-type. The Fluency in Questioning Guide asks the user to decide the value of some items and the frequency of others. It is roughly halfway between the Classroom Guidance Schedule and Pupil Reinforcement Guide. The other guides used in the programme also may be placed in the P-/A-type model. This is a useful preliminary exercise to planning your own methods of observing teaching.

Seven points on the use of rating guides in microteaching

All the rating guides in this skills programme have been examined for reliability and validity when used by supervisors and students at the New University of Ulster. It must be emphasized that the measuring instrument is not the rating guide but the rater. It is therefore important to follow an agreed set of rules when rating teaching. If you also want to gain maximum benefit from the teaching skill practice you should pay particular attention to Step 1 below.

1. Read the appropriate guide before you plan the lesson.
2. Read it again just before you view your lesson.
3. Bear in mind the items of the guide whilst you view the lesson.
4. Jot down your impressions during viewing.

PUPIL REINFORCEMENT

Please read this guide before you teach, and before you view
your microlesson. When rating your lesson place a tick in the
appropriate column.

	Rarely	Sometimes	Almost always
1. You responded to pupil answers and questions with such words as good, fine, splendid			
2. You encouraged pupils to participate by using cues such as ah ha, mmmm, mm'mm, etc.			
6. You gave credit for the correct part of a pupil's answer			
7. You linked pupils' responses to other pupil responses made earlier in the lesson			

FLUENCY IN ASKING QUESTIONS

Please read this schedule before planning and teaching your
microlesson on questioning and immediately before viewing your
lesson.

Ring the appropriate word

1. Your questions were usually clearly
   understood by the pupils   Yes   No

2. Your questions were usually coherently
   expressed   Yes   No

3. You used pauses after asking most of
   your questions   Yes   No

8. You used probing techniques to help pupils
   think more deeply about their answers   Yes   No

9. You used a variety of lower order and
   higher order questions   Yes   No

5. At the end of viewing decide whether your performance on the first item was poor (−) or good (+). If, and only if, you cannot decide use the midpoint 4.
6. Repeat the process for each item. Pause between items to avoid judgements on one item contaminating judgement on the next.
7. Justify your rating on each item with specific illustrations from the lesson whenever possible.

These procedures will help you to be consistent. If you also view, rate and discuss your ratings with other team members you will gradually arrive at a consensus. I usually ask my teams of students to write a P-type report on themselves and each other at the end of the skills programmes. Their reports are often remarkably perceptive. The contents of these reports are not revealed to the other team members.

Activity 15

1. Rate your first microteaching lessons (Activities 2 and 8) on the Classroom Guidance Schedule.
2. Ask another member/other members of the team to rate them.
3. Discuss your ratings of each other's first lessons.
4. Keep the Classroom Guidance Schedule with your first lesson notes in your Teaching Studies folder.

Note: At the end of the skills programme you will be asked to rate both your first lesson with pupils (Activity 11) and your final lesson. The team member(s) should also do this exercise with you.

Unit IV · Perceiving teaching by A-type methods

Analytical methods of observing teaching

Rating schedules are easy to use. They are helpful, quite informative and, if they are used in the way indicated in the previous unit, they are reliable. Their disadvantage is that you lose virtually all the information of the lesson's structure, interactions and content. Rating schedules are usually based upon relatively high inference and loosely structured variables. They reduce a large number and variety of teaching behaviours to points on a set of scales.

In contrast, A-type methods are usually based upon tightly structured variables of relatively low inference (see Rosenshine and Furst, 1973). Examples are 'teacher asks questions', 'pupil replies', 'pupil asks question', teacher uses pupil ideas'. Two approaches may be distinguished, signs and categories. Both are systematic observation systems which focus upon teacher–pupil interactions and both retain more information than rating schedules. Non-verbal and verbal sign and category systems are available. Simon and Boyer (1970) list ninety-two and there are at least another fifty in existence. In a sign system an event is recorded only once if it occurs in a specified time period. When an event is recorded each time it occurs then a category system is being used. The distinction between signs and categories blurs as you narrow the time interval or widen your definition of an event. The items from the Fluency in Questioning Guide given in the previous unit can be converted into a sign system by dropping words such as 'usually' and recording the occurrence of the behaviour every half minute. The Pupil Reinforcement Guide may also be changed to a sign or category system.

Introducing BIAS

A-type methods have to be learnt. Some of the more sophisticated systems such as OSCAR or the Galloway system of non-verbal communication require at least twelve hours' training. (Medley and Mitzel, 1963; Galloway, 1969). Throughout this programme you will be using an all purpose category system devised by the author, Brown's Interaction Analysis System or BIAS. It is unashamedly biased towards verbal interaction of teacher and pupils and it displays the patterns of interaction which occur in a lesson. It was designed for use by teams of students and teachers in microteaching. It takes about two to three hours to learn the basic techniques and you should preferably do this in three or four stints plus some private study – otherwise you may get confused. Five teams of four students seeems to be an optimal group size.

Below are set out the main categories, which you should spend two minutes reading and learning. You will note that TL is a large category. Later on you will be learning some extensions of TL and the other categories. For the moment stick to learning the system, not evaluating it.

The categories of BIAS are fairly clear-cut provided that you remember that what determines the category are intentions and knowledge not grammatical structures. Here are a few examples:

1. In a lesson on plants and animals on a nearby shore, one nine-year-old pupil said, 'Do you mean, miss, it's like an ecosystem?' This would be coded PV because one does not expect nine-year-olds to know and use this term nor did the teacher intend to draw this conceptual point so succinctly from the class. The same remark by a sixth former in a grammar school could legitimately be coded as PR.
2. 'Peter, tell us a bit more about that' is a question (TQ) not a direction (TL).
3. 'Peter, will you please close the window' is a direction (TL) not a question (TQ).
4. 'Peter, will you please shut up' is a reprimand (X) not a question.
5. 'That's not quite correct, Peter' is a mild criticism (TR) not a reprimand (X).
6. 'Well, what are the five main points about the Civil War? They are . . .' This type is usually part of a description (TL) not a question. The context and speed of delivery are important clues.

The BIAS Categories

TL *Teacher lectures* – describes, explains, narrates, directs

TQ *Teacher questions* about content or procedure which pupils are intended to answer.

TR *Teacher responds* – Accepts feelings of the class; describes past feelings and future feelings in a non-threatening way. Praises, encourages, jokes *with* pupils. Accepts or uses pupils' ideas. Builds upon pupil responses. Uses mild criticism such as 'no, not quite'.

PR *Pupils respond directly and predictably* to teacher questions and directions.

PV *Pupils volunteer* information, comments or questions.

S *Silence*, Pauses, short periods of silence.

X *Unclassifiable*. Confusion in which communications cannot be understood. Unusual activities such as reprimanding or criticizing pupils. Demonstrating without accompanying teacher or pupil talk. Short spates of blackboard work without accompanying teacher or pupil talk.

Note: The system was designed for use during verbal exchanges. It is wasteful to use it for other activities such as class tests, copying notes for long periods, individual pupil learning, play acting.

You will not always agree on difficult cases, particularly those on the PV/PR border. In cases of doubt, code as PV. When doubtful about use of pupil ideas or use of teacher ideas code as TR. If 'mild criticism' or 'reprimand' is difficult, code as X.

It is important to learn BIAS with other colleagues so that you can discuss coding difficulties and if necessary establish your own ground rules.

Activity 16

Read the description of categories again. Categorize the following communications without looking at the description of categories. If you get stuck, go back at the end of each section and read the categories again. Compare and discuss your answers with other team members. Some of the items are difficult to agree upon. *My suggested answers are given at the end of the book.*

Section 1
1. TEACHER "Mary, what on earth are you doing?'
2. TEACHER 'My word, you are bubbly today. What have you just been doing?' (*At the beginning of a lesson.*)
3. TEACHER 'Susan, tell the class what the homework is about.' (*Just after the teacher has explained the homework.*)
4. TEACHER 'That's a good idea, John.'
5. TEACHER 'Mm that's splendid.'
6. TEACHER 'You are not quite on target.' (*Said in a matter of fact tone.*)
7. TEACHER 'That's absolute rubbish.'
8. TEACHER 'I'm ashamed of you. How could you . . .'
9. PUPIL 'Please, sir, I've finished.'
10. PUPIL 'Please, sir, can I leave the room?'
11. PUPIL 'Why do we have to do these?'
12. •PUPIL 'Sir, I can't do this one.'
13. PUPIL 'Is it Lagos?'
14. STUDENT 'What's this to do with learning to teach?'

Section 2
Now try these. Write down the appropriate category after every stroke (/). Remember to code on the stroke not on everything which comes before it. Look at intentions, not grammar.

TEACHER. Last time we met, you told me about the stories of Geoffrey Chaucer /[1] Can anyone remember the name of one of his stories? /[2] (*Silence*) /[3]

TEACHER. Well, can anyone remember the names of any of the people in the stories? /[4] (*Silence*) /[5]

PUPIL. (*Hesitatingly*) Miss, I don't think you told us the names of the stories. /[6]

TEACHER. Didn't I? (*Silence*) /[7] Oh! I see your problem /[8] They don't seem to have any names. /[9]

PUPIL. (*in chorus*) Yeees!
TEACHER. That was silly of me. /¹⁰ Susan, tell us the name of one of
    the tales. /¹¹
PUPIL. Was there 'A Reeves Tale'? /¹²
TEACHER. Yes. That's an interesting one. /¹³ What made you remember
    that one, Susan? /¹⁴

Section 3
Read Section 2 again. It was the opening of a student's second lesson.
Rewrite the teacher and pupil communications and then pass them to
a colleague to code.
For your information, the teacher was discussing *The Canterbury Tales.*
Their titles are simply *The Miller's Tale, The Franklin's Tale, The Knight's
Tale,* etc. Hence the confusion of this group of ten-year-olds.

Discuss the codings with your colleague.

Using the time-line display sheets

You should now be able to identify the BIAS categories in most tapescripts of lessons. This section describes how to record microlessons on the time-line display sheets. The next activity teaches you how to use the display. Subsequent activities move you towards being able to record live lessons. Be prepared for some frustrations during these activities.

Figure 8 sets out a time-line display sheet. For your convenience a summary of the main categories is given at the head of the sheet. You record the appropriate category in every successive column. The basic mark to use is / (if you are left handed). Other codes are given later. The categories are grouped into teacher talk, pupil talk, silenceI and unclassifiable. Always begin with a mark in the X row. (Some students say this is because the way I begin teaching is always unclassifiable.) The order of categories has been arranged to minimize hand movements. Eventually lessons begin to have a recognizable 'feel' or pattern about them. If an unclassifiable period extends over two time intervals or more you should scribble down what is happening (e.g. 'b – blackboard work'). If a tiny but critical incident occurs such as a pupil grabbing the teacher's coat sleeve, note it. Coding is easier in pencil. At the end of the lesson turn the BIAS recording sheets over and jot down a brief description of what you saw and felt (P-type observation). This is most important when you are recording BIAS on other people's lessons. Before tackling the next assignment, look at the time-line display in Figure 8, and invent a short sequence which would roughly fit the time-line display.

Figure 8. Brown's Interaction Analysis System (BIAS)

TL = Teacher describes, explains, narrates, directs
TQ = Teacher questions
TR = Teacher responds to pupil's response
PR = Pupil's response to teacher's questions

PV = Pupil volunteers information, comments or questions
S = Silence
X = Unclassifiable

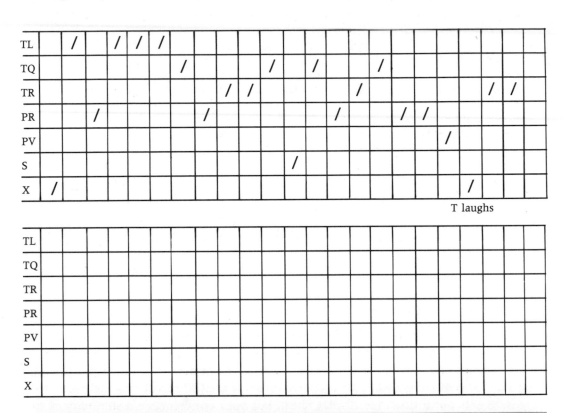

T laughs

Activity 17

Reread the previous two sections and then analyse the following tape script without referring to the detailed description of the categories. / indicates the end of the coding interval. Put a mark in the appropriate row of the time-line display. (Suggested answers are given at the end on page 147.)

Section 1

TEACHER. /¹ Good morning, ladies and gentlemen. /² Today I am going to introduce you to interaction analysis. /³ Interaction analysis is a technique of analysing /⁴ the behaviour of teacher and pupils in classrooms and other teaching situations. /⁵ There are many ways of doing this. /⁶ One can simply give a mark /⁷ or a global rating. One can use rating schedules or plus minus sign systems. /⁸ One can use category systems which permit time-line displays. /⁹ One can even use multiple category systems in which a teaching event /¹⁰ is classified in several different ways. The latter are cumbersome to use /¹¹ and usually not very helpful to teachers or teacher educators. /¹² Most category systems are based upon verbal behaviour /¹³ although some focus upon non-verbal behaviour /¹⁴ such as smiles, eye contact, hand movements, body movements, etc., etc. /¹⁵ All category systems are a little difficult to learn at first. /¹⁶ I am going to introduce you to one which is called BIAS. /¹⁷ BIAS is an abbreviation of Brown's Interaction Analysis System. /¹⁸ It is easy to use.

STUDENT. Excuse me, sir. /¹⁹

TEACHER. Yes, Patrick. /²⁰

STUDENT. You said just now that all category systems are difficult to learn /²¹ and then you said BIAS was easy. /²² How can something be difficult and easy at the same time? /²³

TEACHER. (Laughs in a friendly way.) /²⁴ Well Patrick, you've not quite got the idea. /²⁵ When you are learning BIAS you may get confused but after /²⁶ you have practised it for one hour it becomes very easy. /²⁷ Do you get it now? /²⁸

STUDENT. Mm, all right, I see now. /²⁹

Section 2

Now try this extract from a microlesson. It contains some difficult items. Discuss the time-line displays with your colleagues and arrive at an agreement about any controversial items. (STUDENT = student teacher) Remember to code on the interval, not on everything which comes before it. Start with an X.

STUDENT. /¹ (Smiles) Well since this is the first time we have met /² we had better introduce ourselves. My name /³ is Miss Alexander. What's your name? /⁴ (Student points.)

PUPIL. Andrew, Andrew McEvoy. /⁵

STUDENT. Where do you live, Andrew? /⁶

PUPIL. In Portrush Road, miss./⁷

STUDENT. Oh, yes. That's in Portstewart, isn't it? Does anyone else live /⁸ in Portrush Road?

Student continues to get to know her microclass of eight-to nine-year-olds and where they live. She then says:)
STUDENT. Susan. Which road is your school in? /[9]
(Silence. /[10] Student waits. Some pupils put up their hands. /[11])
STUDENT. Billy, you tell us. /[12]
PUPIL. Central Avenue, miss. /[13]
(Another pupil raises her hand.)
STUDENT. Yes, Fiona. /[14]
PUPIL. (Shyly) Miss. Our school is in two roads? /[15]
STUDENT. (Sounds puzzled) Is it Fiona? Tell me about it. /[16]
PUPIL. (Wriggles in her seat) Well you see, Miss. There's Central Avenue /[17]
    and there's Queenora Avenue and our school is on the /[18] corner.
STUDENT. You mean it's like this? /[19] (Student draws on board as she is
    speaking.) Pupils nod. Two say 'Yes' in quiet voices. /[20])
STUDENT. Well, that's very helpful Fiona. /[21] I'm glad you told us that
    because I want to show you a wee map. /[22]
(Student walks over to a side desk, picks up a drawing board on which
is pinned a schematic map of the school and neighbourhood. /[24])
STUDENT. Sammy. Show us where you live. /[24]
PUPIL. (Sammy points to his road). 'There, miss' /[25]
STUDENT. Now, Fiona . . . /[26]
PUPIL. (Fiona points to her street) 'It's the end of here, miss' /[27]
PUPIL. My street isn't on your map. /[28]
STUDENT. Oh, isn't it Jimmy. Where /[29] do you live?
PUPIL. Prospect Road. /[30]
STUDENT. Prospect Road. Where about's that? Show us roughly on the
    map./[31]
(Jimmy stares hard at the map and points to unmapped area to the right
of the map. /[32]
STUDENT. Oh, you mean it's past /[33] the convent?
PUPIL. Yes. /[34]
STUDENT. Well next week, I'll bring a bigger map /[35] and you can show
    me exactly where you live. /[36]

Coding at three-second intervals

You will by now have discovered that BIAS or indeed any interaction analysis system involves making inferences. There is no such thing as one hundred per cent agreement in the use of A-type methods. Inevitably if you focus upon some activities then you exclude others. Similarly if you code at three-second intervals then you miss out what happens at 0·1 second intervals. The picture you construct using A-type methods is sparser than the reality, but it is clear.

In the next activity you are going to code a tapescript read aloud by one of your team. Three-second intervals are used for coding. Ten or five second intervals prove to be more difficult than three seconds because so many things can happen in the time interval that judgement of what is happening at the end of the interval is difficult. If you don't believe this, try ten or five second intervals. Two second intervals are too short for most people. You should have available a three second bleep on an audio tape recorder. If this is not possible one of the team should tap the desk every third second. If he hasn't a stop watch he should mutter to himself slowly 101, 202, 303, code, 101, 202, 303. Observers have a tendency to speed up when the teacher talks quickly and slow down when the teacher talks slowly. It is better to keep to a regular rhythm independent of the teacher's speed of delivery. Some BIAS users have pointed out that if you code exactly *on* the three second interval, then slow speaking teachers may appear to have unusual gaps in their talk or not be saying anything for much of the time. If the teacher is that slow in speaking, he probably appears that slow to his pupils so still code him according to the rules. After looking at the time-line display he may decide to change his rate of speaking.

Activity 18

You need a three second bleep or stop watch for this activity and any further activities in this book involving BIAS. Turn back to pp. 54–9 of the previous unit. A member of the team should read the tapescript of the two microlessons fairly slowly and expressively whilst the remainder record the time-line display. In cases of doubt leave a blank rather than frantically attempt to catch up with the three second interval.

Compare your time-line displays. They will almost certainly differ marginally — what is important is whether the overall pattern of events is roughly the same. Highly trained observers usually get about 85 per cent agreement on total categories. After two to three hours of BIAS training you can expect about 70 to 75 per cent agreement.

After discussing the BIAS time-line displays, repeat the exercise with another team member reading the lessons expressively. Again compare and discuss your time-line displays. Then compare the two sets of time-line displays from the two different readings. You will find differences between the readings due partly to you as rater and partly to the delivery of the speakers.

Note: Students who have done this exercise prefer to read the tapescripts for themselves rather than use audio tape recordings. Discussion is usually much more lively after the students have read the scripts than after listening to tape recordings.

Activity 19

Each member of the team should teach for *two* minutes to the other members of the team. Videorecord the lessons. Use BIAS to analyse each lesson in turn. Remember to jot down your impressions of the lesson immediately after completing BIAS. Discuss any coding problems which arose in each lesson before moving on to the next lesson.

Notes: 1. Videorecording is not absolutely necessary if you have enough people to play the pupil roles whilst others observe. Students seem to prefer this approach to videorecording.

2. Here is an interesting variation which a supervisor may use in the above activity if he is working with two or more teams together. Ask some of the students privately to plan their lessons before coming to the BIAS class *and not to tell anyone else or use lesson notes in the lesson.* Call upon these students and other students who have not been given this instruction. At the end of the training session ask the students to look at the time-line displays and decide which lessons were planned and which were not. If the team members are experienced teachers they should *all* be asked to teach something they have not taught before. It is usually easy to spot the unplanned lessons of students from the BIAS analyses. It is, of course, more difficult to spot unplanned lessons of experienced teachers since they have already acquired a repertoire of skills and knowledge.

Some clues to look for are given at the end of the book (p. 147).

Extending BIAS

BIAS captures the general pattern of a lesson. When you have mastered the basic BIAS you can extend its use for particular analyses by using letters instead of or in addition to the stroke marks. If you are interested in distinguishing the frequency of individual pupil contributions a large stroke / can be used to separate them. If you are interested in identifying individual pupil's contributions use a different number for each pupil. All extensions of BIAS require extra training. You should avoid using several extensions simultaneously until you are a very highly skilled observer. Focus on the extensions which are relevant. If the lessons under review have been videorecorded they may be analysed in several different ways.

I have set out below a few extensions of BIAS which we have found useful. You can develop your own extensions, but be wary of producing several extensions to one category and of ambiguities in your extensions. Simon and Boyer's (1967) review of instruments, and Flanders (1970) will prove helpful if you are wishing to develop new categories.

TEACHER LECTURES: If interested in time spent reading or story telling, use r (reading), s (story telling) and code the remainder of the category as a stroke /.

TEACHER QUESTIONS: If interested in cognitive level of questions used mark l (lower order) of h (higher order). See unit VI for further details. If interested in probes and prompts use p. Do not use l, h, p, together. They overlap.

TEACHER RESPONDS: You may want to distinguish between simple praise, use of pupils' ideas and *mild* criticism. r (rewards), u (uses pupils' ideas), c (mild criticism) are appropriate letters.

PUPIL RESPONDS: To distinguish incorrect or incomplete responses use e (error).

PUPIL VOLUNTEERS: Use c for comments, observations. h for requests for help. q for questions.

SILENCE: Use r for rapt attention, a for astonished, p for puzzled.

UNCLASSIFIABLE: Use b for unaccompanied blackboard work, p for individual pupil learning, i for interruption by a visitor, d for disruption such as paint being spilt, l for laughter. Remember to scribble note on any unclassifiable activity which is unusual or goes on for more than six seconds.

Interpreting BIAS

Now you have got the feel of BIAS let us look at the two basic ways of interpreting the data. The first uses the frequency of each category, the second uses the time-line display of categories.

Category frequencies

Total the frequencies of each category and calculate the percentage frequencies. If you only want a rough guide, for a ten minute lesson divide each category total by 2. Set out a distribution table and a histogram based upon the percentages. Two examples are given below (see Figure 9). They are based upon a student's first and second lessons in the microteaching programme. Each lesson was of ten minutes' duration. The figures have been rounded off to the nearest ten so you can see the patterns more clearly. Percentage frequencies are given in brackets.

In the first lesson this student talked for 75 per cent of the time, 20 per cent of the time was taken up with questions. She only received pupil responses for 10 per cent of the time and 15 per cent of the time was recorded as silence. After viewing her lesson and seeing the BIAS analysis, she planned a lesson and taught it. In that lesson she talked for 70 per cent of the time of which 15 per cent were questions. On this occasion she received pupil responses for 20 per cent of the time and a further 5 per cent of pupil voluntary contributions. Silence was reduced from 15 to 5 per cent.

The statistical descriptions can be formalized and expressed as percentages of the total number of interactions or as ratios of the number of interactions within various categories. The most useful are percentage teacher talk; percentage pupil talk; percentage

Figure 9. Example of BIAS frequencies

	TL	TQ	TR	PR	PV	S	X	Totals
Lesson 1	100(50%)	40(20%)	10(5%)	20(10%)	0(0%)	30(15%)	0(0%)	200
Lesson 2	70(35%)	30(15%)	40(20%)	40(20%)	10(5%)	10(5%)	0(0%)	200

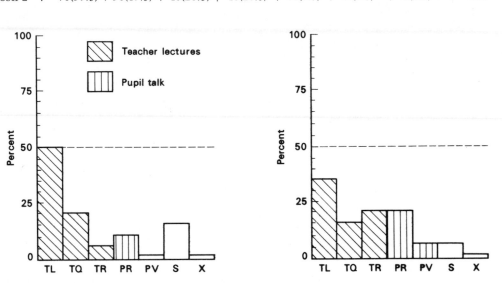

silence; percentage unclassifiable. Useful ratios are teacher question / pupil response; teacher response / pupil response; teacher response / pupil voluntary response; teacher response / total pupil talk; teacher talk / pupil talk; teacher lecture / pupil talk; and teacher lecture / silence. These ratios indicate the nature of the lesson. A high teacher question / pupil response ratio is usually to be avoided; a high teacher lectures / pupil talk ratio in a discussion lesson is clearly undesirable. A low teacher response / pupil talk ratio is important in discussion lessons.

Using the time-line display

There are two features of time-line displays to look for. Steady states in which the same category is sustained for more than two or three intervals and patterns. A TQ which extends over three intervals is likely to be very complex, confused or a string of questions with no opportunity for pupils to answer. A string of PRs or PVs which follow a TQ and an S is usually a healthy sign in a discussion lesson. A string of PVs immediate after TLs suggests the existence of control or communication difficulties.

More revealing and interesting are the patterns which can occur in different types of lessons and curriculum areas. Before reading the description which follows each example you might like to try guessing what kind of lesson the pattern occurs in.

Example 1

TL		/	/										
TQ				/		/		/		/			
TR													
PR					/		/		/		/		
PV													
S													
X	/												

This is a drill type lesson. It occurs in simple arithmetic, and foreign language teaching and revision.

Example 2

TL	/	/	/				/	/			
TQ				/					/		
TR						/					
PR					/					/	
PV											
S											
X											

This is the most common pattern occurring in any lesson in any curriculum area. Brief teacher lectures followed by a question, a brief pupil response, a teacher response and more teacher talk.

Example 3

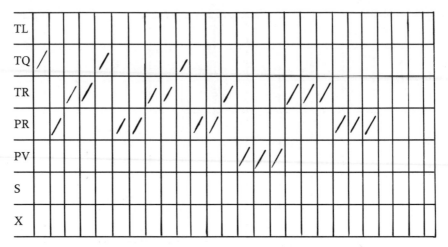

This is a fairly common pattern in English lessons. The sustained TRs usually bring forth PVs as well as PRs which the teacher then builds on.

Example 4

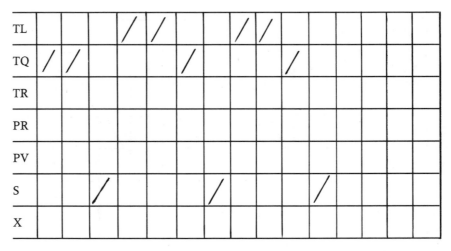

A beginner's lesson. Notice how he questions, receives no answer and rushes in with TLs. His pupils may be manipulating his behaviour. They keep quiet and he answers his own questions. This pattern then reinforces their silence keeping.

Example 5

TL										/	/				
TQ	/	/	/		/	/		/							
TR															
PR															
PV															
S				/			/		/						
X															

A variation of Example 4. When no answer is forthcoming, the teacher rushes in with more questions. In the end he answers them himself.

Example 6 – using the extension l = lower order, h = higher order questioning (see Unit VI):

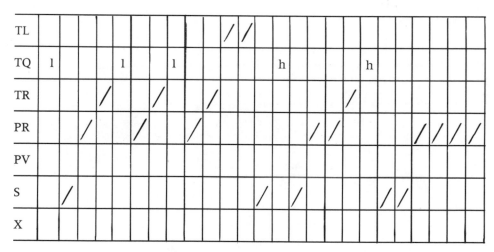

An example of the beginning of a high level discussion lesson in science. Teacher begins with lower order (factual) questions, responds to pupils, talks, pauses before asking a high level question and afterwards. Asks higher order (thought) question again, pauses longer and obtains sustained pupil responses.

Example 7 (The X's have not been labelled to make it harder)

TL	/	/									/				
TQ												/			
TR															/
PR													/		
PV				/	/										
S									/	/					
X						/	/	/							

The missing label is r, reprimanded. The pupils called out, the teacher reprimanded, there was silence, a direction, a question, a pupil response and a teacher response. Once this pattern occurs in a particular lesson, it is likely to occur again unless there are frequent strings of TRs and brief TLs (directions).

Activity 20

(Remember to have a 3-second bleep or stop watch available for 3. below)

1. Obtain a frequency count from the time-line displays you made in Activity 17. Draw the histograms based upon the percentages of each category and compare them.
2. Obtain a frequency count from one of the time-line displays of each lesson that you made in Activity 18. Draw the histograms based upon the percentages of each category and compare them. Work out the teacher lectures: pupil talk ratio, the TR/PR + PV ratio for each lesson.
3. Apply BIAS to your very first lesson (Activity 2), and your planned lesson (Activity 8). Obtain frequency counts and draw the histograms based upon the percentages of each category. (In ten minute lessons, percentages may be obtained by dividing categories total by 2.) Search for any repeated patterns in the lessons. Write a brief comparison of the lesson based upon your BIAS analysis.

Retain in your folder. (The videorecordings of Activities 2 and 8 may now be erased.)

BIAS as a simple teaching model

The categories and time-line displays of the system not only describe what happens in a lesson but it can also be used to describe what you want to happen in a lesson. Thus BIAS may serve as a simple teaching model. Suppose for example you want to gain more pupil participation than you did in a previous lesson. Increase the TRs, particularly the use of pupils' ideas, and try again. The time-line display and frequency count will tell you how successful you have been. Similarly try a TQ followed by five Ss to see if this evokes a PR, and try sustained TRs – rewards, and use of pupils' ideas – to see if this evokes PRs. These are just some of the ways in which BIAS can be used. As you progress through the skill training you will discover others.

We have now come to the end of your training in BIAS. As you have seen, it may be used to analyse lessons, categories may be extended and it may be used as a teaching model. Its main use in this programme is as a sharply defined feedback instrument. To be told by a P-type observer that you ask too many questions and you are hesitant is not as meaningful or as precise as being told by an A-type observer that BIAS indicates you spent 40 per cent of the time asking questions, received answers only 25 per cent of the time and three-quarters of the silences occurred within your lecturing. When you are your own observer the results can become a potent challenge to improve.

The work of N. A. Flanders

BIAS was derived from a well-known and most important system known as FIAC (Flander's Interaction Categories). This system was developed by the leading expert on classroom interaction, Ned Flanders, in the late 'fifties and early 'sixties. It has at least twenty offspring. Some use several sub-categories and some, such as BIAS, use fewer categories. Recent developments in the use of FIAC are reported in Flanders (1970) and he is at present developing a modified form of FIAC for use in the Far West Laboratory Minicourses (self instruction courses for practising teachers). Flanders' basic ten category system is given on page 82.

His basic system may be used as a simple category count, a time-line display or in the form of 10 × 10 matrices. The matrix is constructed from the frequency counts of overlapping, consecutive pairs of numbers obtained in the lesson observation. For example, the string of numbers 10–1–5–5–5–4–8–2–4–8 would be coded as 10,1; 1,5; 1,5; 1,5; 5,4; 4,8; 8,2; 2,4; 4,8. The frequency of these pairs of number are then plotted in the matrix. The matrix is then used to calculate ratios and examine steady states (the same category used over more than one time interval) and transitions.

Figure 10 sets out the main areas of interest in Flanders' matrix. It is a valuable research tool but it is very time consuming unless one has computer facilities. It takes about two hours to construct by hand a matrix from the coding of a ten minute lesson. Table 2 sets out a matrix of results derived from a recent study by Wragg (Wragg, 1972, 1973). Over 100 post-graduate students at the Department of Education, University of Exeter, were observed at the beginning, middle and end of a term's teaching practice and the results were analysed according to the sex of the teachers, the age range of the pupils, the subjects being taught and the stage of the practice.

Flanders' interaction analysis categories (FIAC)*

Teacher talk	Response	1. *Accepts feeling.* Accepts and clarifies an attitude or the feeling tone of a pupil in a non-threatening manner. Feelings may be positive or negative. Predicting and recalling feelings are included. 2. *Praises or encourages.* Praises or encourages pupil action or behaviour. Jokes that release tension, but not at the expense of another individual; nodding head, or saying 'Um hm?' or 'Go on' are included. 3. *Accepts or uses ideas of pupils.* Clarifying, building or developing ideas suggested by a pupil. Teacher extensions of pupil ideas are included but as the teacher brings more of his own ideas into play, shift to category 5.
		4. *Asks questions.* Asking a question about content or procedure, based on teacher ideas, with the intent that a pupil will answer.
	Initiation	5. *Lecturing.* Giving facts or opinions about content or procedures; expressing *his own* ideas, giving *his own* explanation, or citing an authority other than the pupil. 6. *Giving directions.* Directions, commands, or orders to which a pupil is expected to comply. 7. *Criticizing or justifying authority.* Statements intended to change pupil behaviour from non-acceptable to acceptable pattern; bawling someone out; stating why the teacher is doing what he is doing; extreme self-reference.
Pupil talk	Response	8. *Pupil talk-response.* Talk by pupils in response to teacher. Teacher initiates the contact or solicits pupil statement or structures the situation. Freedom to express own ideas is limited.
	Initiation	9. *Pupil talk – initiation.* Talk by pupils which they initiate. Expressing own ideas; initiating a new topic; freedom to develop opinions and a line of thought, like asking thoughtful questions going beyond the existing structure.
Silence		10. *Silence or confusion.* Pauses, short periods of silence and periods of confusion in which communication cannot be understood by the observer.

*There is *no* scale implied by these numbers. Each number is classificatory; it designates a particular kind of communication event. To write these numbers down during observation is to enumerate not to judge a position on a scale.

Reprinted by permission of Professor N. A. Flanders from *Analysing Teaching Behaviour* (Addison-Wesley, 1970), p. 34.

Figure 10. Key to Flanders' Matrix   [83]

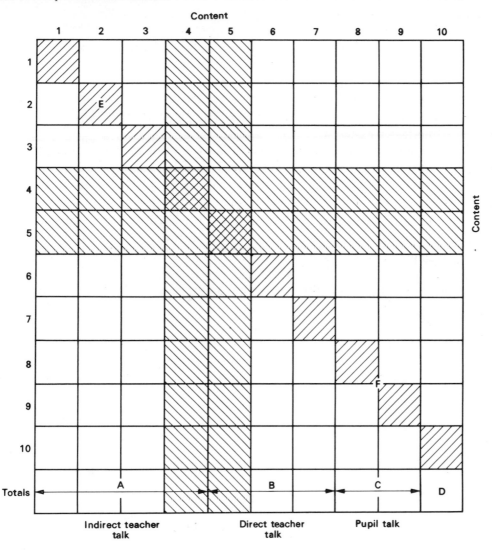

Notes
Cells are given in conventional form: row, column order
All observations begin and end with 10, (0)
Example : The sequences 10.3–6– . . . are recorded
          in matrix in cell 10,3 ; cell 3,6 etc.
          in overlapping pairs.

A = indirect teacher talk   E = sustained teacher praise and use of ideas
B = direct teacher talk   F = sustained pupil talk
C = pupil talk   ▨ = Steady State cells – categories sustained for 3 seconds
D = silence   ▧ = Content cross cell*

* Content cross cell = area of extended influence. Based on assumption that most of lesson content is
  category 4 (questions) and 5 (lectures).

As you can see from the matrix most of the tallies occur within the content cross and there are relatively few in the area of extended influence (see Key to Flanders' Matrix). A matrix of primary school lessons tallies would probably yield fewer 5,5s, more 4,8s and possibly more 3,9s. About 65 per cent of the lessons observed were devoted to talk and 73 per cent of this was teacher talk. This leaves very little for individual pupil contributions. Compared with experienced teachers in the United States, this group of British student teachers tended to use lecture, accepting and praising more and questions, commands and criticisms less. The British pupils initiated more talk than their American counterparts.

The analysis did not reveal distinctive teaching styles associated with different subjects but certain patterns were more likely to occur in some subjects rather than others. For example, 5–5–5–10–10–10–10 (dictation) occurred in Chemistry but rarely in English. The chain 9–9–9–9–9–5–5–9–9–9 (discussion) occurred most often in English and never in Mathematics. No clear cut changes occurred during the practice but by the end of the practice, the amount of continuous lecturing had dropped substantially and there was greater use of silence (work activities), fewer questions were asked and less praise was used.

The results of Flanders and other interaction analyses have also been related to pupil

Matrix for all teachers (337,617 tallies from 578 lessons)

	1	2	3	4	5	6	7	8	9	10	Total	
1	0	0	0	0	0	0	0	0	0	0	0	Accepts feeling
2	0	1	3	3	3	1	0	1	2	2	17	Praise
3	0	1	4	8	9	1	0	1	2	3	29	Accepts ideas
4	0	0	0	13	4	1	1	43	2	14	78	Question
5	0	1	0	21	222	7	1	4	17	29	304	Lecture
6	0	0	0	2	4	13	1	5	2	11	38	Command
7	0	0	0	1	2	1	2	1	1	4	12	Criticism
8	0	8	17	12	12	4	2	36	3	6	100	Solicited children's talk
9	0	4	4	4	21	2	2	0	32	5	74	Unsolicited children's talk
10	0	1	0	16	26	9	3	8	12	270	345	Silence or non-codable

Reprinted from 'A study of student teachers in the classroom', in Chanan, G. (1973) *Towards a Science of Teaching* (p. 104), with kind permission of Professor E. C. Wragg.

achievement and attitude measures in the hope of finding teaching patterns which
are universally successful (Flanders and Simon, 1969; Rosenshine, 1971). Beneath the
welter of careful qualifications one finds that probably, enthusiasm, the use of reinforcement, the use of pupils ideas, higher order questioning (for higher order objectives)
and clear explanation are the most important pointers to successful teaching.

You have now completed the basic training in the perception of teaching. You should
be able to recognize, comment on and use a variety of methods of observing teaching
which range from the ostensibly simple P-type to the ostensibly pure A-type. You may
appreciate that truth in these matters is far from pure and never simple and you may
have found that the use of A-type methods has already brought about changes in your
P-type observations and in your teaching.

You should now read the opening paragraphs of the previous unit (pp. 49–50), before
proceeding to the unit on the skills of exposition and listening.

Suggestions for further reading

STONES, E. and MORRIS, S. (1972) *Teaching Practice: Problems and Perspectives,* Methuen.
    (Chapter 7 and the paper by Amidon and Hunter.)
MORRISON, A. and MCINTYRE, D. (eds) (1972) *The Social Psychology of Teaching,* Penguin.
    (Particularly pp. 63–74 and pp. 99–114.)
AMIDON, E. J. and HOUGH, J. B. (eds) (1967) *Interaction Analysis: Theory, Research and Applica-
    tion,* Addison–Wesley. (A series of readings on verbal interaction in the classroom.)
FLANDERS, N. A. (1970) *Analysing Teaching Behaviour,* Addison-Wesley. (A comprehensive test
    which describes in detail the uses and potential of FIAC and related systems.)

Unit V · Exposition and listening

Introduction

This unit is concerned with the skills of exposition and listening. On completing the unit you should be able to identify the main characteristics of set and closure (beginning and ending of lesson topics), teacher liveliness, giving explanations and listening. You should be able to introduce and end your lesson topics in a more effective way, to teach in a lively way and to give more lucid explanations. In addition, you should be able to analyse your exposition and listening skills, and so be able to improve them.

Exposition skills are the core of all the communication skills used in teaching. They all pivot on gaining and holding the attention of the pupil. To achieve this one has to change the levels of stimulation in the teaching situation by: switching to different activities; introducing novel stimuli; varying the pace of the lesson; varying the modulation of the voice; giving a wide range of non-verbal signals such as gestures, facial expressions and body movements, and using the potent weapon of   silence. Even an empty space in a line of print can produce a change of stimulation and puzzle the reader so that he reads on more quickly.

Changes in stimulation, not absolute levels of stimulation, heighten the arousal of the learner. There is now a great deal of physiological evidence that changes in stimulation produce arousal by affecting the reticular activating system of the brain stem (Berlyne, 1962; Lynn, 1966). The changes in stimulation may be from low to high such as when a teacher suddenly shouts, or from high to low such as when a teacher suddenly stops talking. This is particularly attention-gaining if it occurs in the middle of a sentence. The sceptics amongst you should try it for yourselves when you are next talking to one of your friends. Begin a sentence normally and suddenly stop. Your friend will almost certainly react, 'what's the matter?'.

Changes in stimulation will gain and hold attention and it is during the time that you are holding the attention of the learner that he is most likely to learn from you. A skilled and entertaining teacher intuitively uses this device. He may tell a funny story which evokes laughter and noise. When it begins to die down he makes a serious point in a quiet tone of voice and his audience listens carefully. An inexperienced and unskilful teacher often does not know or ignores this principle. Instead of producing a marked change in the stimulation he may simply try to add to it. For example, when a class is very noisy, an inexperienced teacher is likely to frequently shout loudly 'Stop talking' or 'Shut up'. This merely adds to the level of noise, and it may encourage the children to shout even louder. It almost certainly encourages them to ignore the teacher.

What should a teacher do if he finds the class is getting very noisy? What could he do to prevent his class becoming excessively noisy? (See p. 147 for a suggestion.)

Before embarking upon the next sections of the unit you should work out some answers to these questions. They are implicit in the introduction you have just read. They will help you to see the importance of the remainder of the unit.

Set

Those of you who have run in races will be familiar with the starter's instructions: 'On your marks. Get set. Go!' These simple instructions contain the kernel of work on set. In teaching, as in athletics, you have to gain the general attention of the participants, direct them specifically – and see that they go in the right direction.

Set may be technically defined as any device or process which induces a pupil to attend and learn. It directs the learner's attention to a specific task or learning sequence and there is experimental evidence which demonstrates that differences in set induction affect learning outcomes (Aubertine, 1964; Gage, 1972).

Inducing a set to learn also *excludes* the perception and learning of other activities. Some of you will have watches or clocks. Without looking at the watch face, try to recall whether it has all the numbers from 1 to 12 and whether the numbers are in roman or arabic numerals. Now, look quickly at your watch and look away again. Were you correct in your recall? What time was it by your watch? A surprising number of us don't recall correctly because we have never looked carefully at the face of our watches. This shows the importance of attention in learning. Most of us, when we are set on finding the answer to the question about the watch face, do not look at the hands of the watch. This shows how set excludes perception and learning.

It is important to choose the introductory set carefully so that it is interesting in itself to the pupils and there is an obvious link between it and what is to be learnt. A teacher might introduce a lesson on 'fruit' to young pupils by solemnly taking an apple from his pocket and slowly eating it. The novelty of his behaviour would induce a set in his pupils. After eating the apple he might say 'What's this I'm eating?' To which one of the pupils is likely to reply 'An apple, sir.' The teacher might then say 'What's an apple?' The answer 'A fruit, sir' might be given. The teacher could then ask 'What are fruit?' and embark upon a concept lesson on fruit, and their differences from vegetables and nuts. What are the main differences between fruit and vegetables?

Why are children likely to be fascinated by a teacher eating an apple in the class?

Novel introductions to a topic are not always possible. But you should always think carefully about how you introduce a topic – for if your pupils are not attending at the beginning of the learning sequence they are unlikely to begin attending half way through it. Furthermore, if you choose an inappropriate method of inducing set you may find the pupils are not attending to what you want them to attend. I recently saw a lecturer in photography give a talk on contrasting tones and the effects of different kinds of lighting upon photographs. His illustrations were mainly photographs of female figures. The students looked at them attentively. It is unlikely that all of them were listening to his description of colour tones.

[88]   Throughout this section, three different methods of holding the attention of the reader have been used; meaningful examples, analogies and questions. These are also ways of gaining and holding the attention of pupils in classrooms. 'The why, the how and the when' of set induction is given below in a cryptic way so that you can refer to it when planning your microteaching lesson on set (and closure).

Why use set induction
1. To focus student attention on what is to be learnt.
2. To create a frame of reference before or during a lesson.
3. To give meaning to a new concept or principle.
4. To stimulate student interest and involvement.

How to induce a set to learn
1. *Preliminary attention gaining*: Make sure your pupils are attending before you begin. This is best achieved by pausing, looking around the class and waiting until the class is ready. Shouting and bawling lose their effect rapidly.
2. *Orientation*: Select an event, object, process, or device which will interest your pupils, and match your objectives in the lesson. If your choice is too far away from either your pupils' interests or your objectives, then it will block learning and may lead to discipline problems (APPROPRIATE-NESS). Choose something that will provide a structure or focus for your pupils (STRUCTURE).
   Choose something that will help make the objectives of the lesson clear (CLARITY). Analogies, examples and puzzling questions are useful devices.

When to induce a set
1. At the beginning of a lesson.
2. When changing topics.
3. Before a question and answer session.
4. Before a panel discussion.
5. Before films, filmstrips, radio programmes.
There are many other uses. (5) is very important.

Some examples of simple set induction devices
Each of these has been used to induce set:
1. Do something unusual at the beginning of a lesson. For example, emptying one's pockets on to the desk as an introduction to counting and classifying objects.
2. Start a lesson on rhythm by playing a record of drum beats.
3. Using a set of instructions. Example: As you read this report on the Civil War, think about how you could have stopped it if you had (i) a cloak which made you invisible, or (ii) a million pounds.
4. Use an announcement. Example: 'All Moslem children must leave school at noon today. In future no Moslem child can attend school.' This could serve as an introduction to a discussion of freedom of religion.
5. Show them an object and ask questions about it. Example: A machete as an introduction to a lesson on tribal feuds.
6. Ask a provocative question. Example: 'Would you walk down the main street of Scarborough in broad daylight, stark naked, if I gave you £1,000,000 to support starving people in Nigeria? Would you do this, if you could never tell anyone why you did it?' This could be an introduction to a discussion on morality and taboos.
7. Use an analogy (serious or humorous).
8. Use a 'startle' set. Example: Strike a match for a lesson on the importance and dangers of fire to mankind.
   Note: Too many 'startle' sets cease to startle a class. Too strong a startle might disrupt learning.

Activity 21

Plan a simple set induction to any lesson topic of your choice. Outline clearly how you would induce the set to learn and write a brief paragraph indicating how your 'set' is related to the main body of your lesson topic and your lesson objectives. The lesson topic should be suitable for a ten minute microteaching lesson.

Closure

Closure may be technically defined as directing attention to the completion of a specific task or learning sequence. The most commonly used form of closure is the lesson bell announcing the end of a lesson. It is also the most ineffective. Gains in pupil achievement are highest when a summary of the main points are given at the end of a lesson (see Wright and Nuthall, 1970).

There are two important types of closure: cognitive and social. The first is directed at consolidating what the students have learnt and focusing their attention on the major points covered in the lesson or lesson segment. The second is concerned with giving the students a sense of achievement so that, despite any difficulties they encountered within the lesson, they are encouraged to continue striving. Usually, one uses social closure only at the end of a lesson or at the end of a particularly difficult learning sequence.

It is important to know how you hope to end the lesson before you actually begin it so that you and your pupils have a sense of direction and purpose in your lessons. Put baldly, if *you* don't know how to pull together what the pupils have learnt then they probably won't. The cognitive closure should be interesting in itself and, as far as possible, suggest new possibilities and questions. For example, in the previous section of the unit a lesson was sketched in which the teacher began by eating an apple and then went on to develop the concept of 'fruit'. An interesting closure of the end of that lesson would have been to produce a tomato and to ask the class to find out whether that was a fruit or a vegetable. This question requires them to apply their recently learnt knowledge to a new problem. Alternatively the teacher could have completed the lesson by the sentences:

> Well, you've worked hard at this one and, as you say, fruit are produced directly from the blossoms of trees or plants. The next time we meet we'll try to work out how we'd describe a 'vegetable' to a man from another planet.

These sentences contain a brief reference to social closure, cognitive closure and a lead in to the next related topic. The next section sets out formally the main 'Why, when and where' of closure.

Why use cognitive and social closure?
1. To focus attention on what has been learnt.
2. To consolidate pupil learning.
3. To draw attention to the end of a learning sequence.
4. To create a sense of achievement and mastery in the pupils.

When to use cognitive closure
1. At the end of a lesson.
2. At the end of a learning sequence within a lesson.
3. Immediately after a student discussion or practice session.

When to use social closure
1. At the end of a lesson.
2. At the end of a particularly difficult learning sequence.
   (*Note*: Social closure consists of praising and encouraging students.)

Some examples of simple closure devices in different subjects
1. Lesson Topic: Geography.
   'Now let's stop for a little while and go over what we have learnt about the theory of continental drift.'
2. Lesson Topic: writing a book report.
   'Well that's been an interesting discussion about writing reports. Peter put his finger on the key when he said the words "good organization". Now let's list the guide lines. John could you begin?'
3. Lesson topic: Statistics.
   'Well you seem to have learnt how to code and classify objects and draw histograms of them. Could we use histograms to show the class's favourite football teams?'

Activity 22

Design a closure for the topic you planned in Activity 21.

Activity 23

Teach the microlesson you have planned in Activities 21 and 22. Observe your lesson carefully and complete the set and closure appraisal guide given on the next page. Write a brief paragraph (on the lesson record) indicating how you might improve upon your set induction and your cognitive and social closure.

SET AND CLOSURE APPRAISAL GUIDE

Teach/reteach (ring appropriate word)

Name: Topic: Class:

Date: Microteaching supervisor:

Please read the guide before you teach the microlesson, and
look through it whilst you are viewing the teaching session.

Assess your microteaching performance on each of the items rigorously,
as if you were about to qualify as a teacher. Put a ring round the
number which most closely indicates your view of your performance.

7 represents 'truly outstanding' (for a person about to qualify)
and 1 represents 'weak'.

SET

	Interest	NO		YES
1.	Your method of introducing the lesson was in itself interesting	1 2 3	4	5 6 7
2.	Your method of introducing the lesson helped the pupils to become interested in the main part of the lesson	1 2 3	4	5 6 7
	Cognitive link			
3.	The relationship between your introduction and the main part of the lesson was clear to the pupils	1 2 3	4	5 6 7

CLOSURE

	Interest			
4.	Your method of ending the lesson was in itself interesting	1 2 3	4	5 6 7
5.	Your method of ending the lesson reinforced the pupils' interest in the lesson	1 2 3	4	5 6 7
	Cognitive link			
6.	The relationship between your ending and the main part of the lesson was clear to the pupils	1 2 3	4	5 6 7
	Social link			
7.	You created a sense of achievement in your pupils	1 2 3	4	5 6 7

Skill comments:

Teacher liveliness

Of all the skills that you encounter in this course, teacher liveliness is one of the most important. In Unit III (Perceiving Teaching) it was pointed out that Ryan had discovered that 'good' teachers were rated high on stimulating, imaginative behaviour. Rosenshine's (1970) review of studies of teacher enthusiasm and pupil achievement gives clear evidence that enthusiastic lively teachers produce the greatest pupil involvement and learning. The section of the unit is devoted to a discussion of non-verbal and extra-verbal cues and some examples and suggestions on how you might increase your liveliness are given. Non-verbal cues or gestures refer to the signals we give with our bodies. These essentially consist of eye movements, facial expressions, gestures, head and body movements (Argyle, 1970). The non-verbal cues convey emotions and feelings and they qualify the verbal cues we are giving. For example, the phrase 'You are a rogue' when uttered with a fiery glare has a different meaning from the same phrase uttered with a friendly smile.

Extra-verbal cues refer to voice tone and quality, and the grunts and noises we make. These cues convey emotions and feelings and qualify the verbal cues. For example, 'Mmmmm! *You're* a nice girl' is different in meaning from, 'Hmph. You're a *nice* girl.'

Non-verbal and extra-verbal cues are the main constituents of teacher liveliness. Teacher liveliness basically consists of changing the patterns of stimulation of the learner so that his attention is gained and held. Most of you will have attended at least one boring lecture. If you analyse the cues a boring lecturer uses, you will find that they are few, that he is limited in his movements, he rarely changes his facial expression, there is an absence of gesture, often a surfeit of 'ums' and 'ahs' and he speaks in a dull flat monotonous voice. Even the most dull and boring teacher or lecturer can improve provided he pays attention to the following elements.

TEACHER MOVEMENT

When you are holding a question and answer session you should stand a little way from the blackboard so that you have to change your position to write. If you are talking to small group of pupils in the class, you should move gently towards them. If you wish to observe the whole class move slowly towards the back wall so that eventually you can see the pupils but they cannot see you. All of the above compel the pupils to make sensory adjustments so that their attention is likely to be gained. Sudden body movements or sudden stops rapidly gain the attention of pupils and they are useful as control techniques.

The way you move towards a pupil conveys meaning to him. Work out how a teacher should move towards a pupil to convey friendliness, and to convey hostility.

TEACHER GESTURE

Gestures of the hands, body and face all convey meaning. If you nod very quickly in Britain it usually means 'Yes. I know that. Please continue quickly.' If you raise your eyebrows as far as they will go it means 'I am astonished.' If you raise them slightly it means 'Please continue talking.'

The above are but a few of the many gestures one uses in communication. A useful game to play is to see how long you keep a person talking by using gestures and sounds but not words.

EYE CONTACT AND MOVEMENT

Eye movements and contact are a key way of conveying emotions and controlling interaction. If you stare very hard at someone whilst you are talking to him, it is difficult for him to interrupt you. If you stare at every part of his body except his face whilst he is talking to you, it is difficult for him to concentrate on what he is saying, If a person opens his eyes wide he is usually saying 'That's interesting,' if he opens them very wide, he is usually saying 'That's alarming.' If a girl looks at a boy and quickly looks down and away as soon as he looks at her she is saying . . . I leave you to decide.

TEACHER VOICE

A dull flat voice leads to a dull flat class. Variations in quality, expressiveness, tone quality and rate of talking all can contribute to teacher liveliness. As an initial step you should try varying the rate of your speaking. You will find that when you change from one speed of talking to another, people will renew their attention in what you are saying.

TEACHER SILENCE

Silence has a language. A short pause before saying something important is an effective way of holding attention. A sudden pause in the middle of a sentence gains attention. A three second pause gains attention. A twenty second pause can be agonizing for an audience. Try reading the above paragraph aloud. Pause every time you come to the word 'pause'.

Beginner teachers tend to be afraid of pauses and silences and rush to fill them with extra questions or statements. An experienced teacher always pauses after he has asked a question, and if he thinks the pupil could extend his answer he may pause again after the pupil stops talking. This usually prompts a pupil to say more. A similar tactic is used by radio and TV interviewers.

On occasions you may want the pupil to pay particular attention to an object or idea. To do this one can use a combination of gestural and verbal focusing. For example, suppose you want to encourage the pupils to read a certain book. You could say in a flat, dull voice 'This book might be interesting to you'. As you are saying this, look at the floor and point feebly at the book.

If you do all this you can rest assured that the majority of pupils will not read the book.

What non-verbal, extra verbal cues and words should you use to arouse the pupils interest in the book? (For suggestions see page 147.)

Focusing is, as you may have guessed, closely related to set. It differs from set in that it does not necessarily link one section of a lesson to another or serve as an introduction to a topic.

We have now completed a brief description of the use of non-verbal and verbal cues which can promote liveliness. Two other main tactics are available for varying stimulation in the classroom.

INTERACTIONS

Some teachers talk too much and therefore lose the attention of their pupils. To avoid this, you should try to use various interaction patterns: teacher–group; teacher–individual pupil; pupil–teacher; and pupil–pupil.

Pupil–pupil interaction is the most difficult to achieve within the confines of the lesson objectives, since pupils tend to look to the teacher to find out whether he approves of their responses. To promote pupil–pupil interaction, one should avoid looking at the pupil who is responding and ask another pupil what he thinks of the first pupil's response. Again, do not look at the pupil who is talking. Instead, look at the first pupil and around the class for anyone who looks as if he is about to speak. If you find someone who seems willing to talk and who is acceptable to the group, ask him for his views. Further details of this subtle skill are contained in Unit VII – Participation in Discussion.

SWITCHING SENSORY CHANNELS

Most of the time teachers use oral and visual cues simultaneously. That is to say, they talk and gesture. One can vary stimulation by using just one of the pupil's sensory channels. For example, one can produce a summary on a chart and say 'Here are the main points', and then remain silent whilst the pupils read the sheet.

One can use other media such as tape recordings, slides, drawings and videotapes so that attention is directed away from the teacher for a short time. When he returns to the scene his words and gestures are more likely to be attended to closely. Such points in a lesson are also good for developing cognitive closure.

Activity 24

1. Set out below are 43 non-verbal cues. Practise them with a friend or supervisor, either in front of a mirror or in front of a video camera.

Non-verbal response repertoire
Non-verbal behaviour

1. Raise eyebrow.
2. Frown.
3. Nod head.
4. Smile.
5. Motion with hand to come nearer.
6. Motion with finger to come nearer.
7. Motion with finger to go away.
8. Motion with hand to go away.
9. Place finger to lip to indicate silence.
10. Cock ear.
11. Extend arm to indicate 'Stop'.
12. Assume 'thinker' pose.
13. Shake head to indicate 'No'.
14. Move from one part of room to another.
15. Point finger at someone.
16. Move hand in circular motion.
17. Hold hands out with palms upward.
18. Point from student to student.
19. Hold chin in hand, look thoughtful.
20. Scratch head.
21. Shift weight from one foot to another.
22. Tap foot.
23. Drum fingers on desk or podium.
24. Tap pencil or pen.
25. Purse lips.
26. Squint eyes.
27. Wink.
28. Tug an ear and look thoughtful.
29. Hold both hands outward as if to ask 'Why?'
30. Fold arms.
31. Put hands on hips.
32. Put hands in pockets.
33. Lean against desk or table.
34. Wrinkle nose.
35. Clap hands together.
36. Clasp hands together.
37. Snap fingers.
38. Bite lower lip.
39. Look at ceiling.
40. Look at floor.
41. Look intently as if at a pupil.
42. Gesture to stand up.
43. Gesture to sit down.

2. Set out below are a list of meanings, feelings and emotions. Practise them with a friend or supervisor, either in front of a mirror or a video camera.

Meanings, feelings, or emotion

1. Satisfaction.
2. Enthusiasm.
3. Tenderness.
4. Kindness.
5. Humour.
6. Interest.

7. Approval.	19. Helplessness.
8. Hope.	20. Indifference.
9. Encouragement.	21. Resignation.
10. Doubt.	22. Noncommittal.
11. Anger.	23. Determination.
12. Defiance.	24. Conviction.
13. Threat.	25. Superiority.
14. Dissatisfaction.	26. Surprise.
15. Impatience.	27. Questioning.
16. Disgust.	28. Puzzlement.
17. Sarcasm.	29. Concentration.
18. Uncertainty.	

3. Select any twelve points out of each of the lists of non-verbal responses, and meanings, feelings and emotions. Try to convey the meaning etc. through non-verbal cues. For example, you might try to convey enthusiasm whilst gesturing to someone to stand up. You may use any additional gestures you like. Write down which non-verbal cue and meaning, feeling or emotion you are trying to convey. Practise with a friend or supervisor, either in front of a mirror or video-camera. Give yourself a rating out of five on each of the problems tackled. The record of this exercise should be kept in your teaching studies folder.

Activity 25

Choose a topic which may be of interest to your pupils. Plan a ten minute microlesson in which you specify the objectives. Incorporate in the lesson the points of teacher liveliness listed in the appraisal guide which follows. Teach the lesson, view it and assign yourself ratings on the guide. Write a brief paragraph indicating in what ways you need to improve your teacher liveliness skills.

TEACHER LIVELINESS APPRAISAL GUIDE

Teach/reteach (ring appropriate word)

Name: Topic: Class:

Date: Microteaching supervisor:

Please read the guide before you teach the microlesson, and
look through it whilst you are viewing the teaching session.

Assess your microteaching performance on each of the items rigorously,
as if you were about to qualify as a teacher. Put a ring round the
number which most closely indicates your view of your performance.

7 represents 'truly outstanding' (for a person about to qualify)
and 1 represents 'weak'.

		NO		YES
1.	**Teacher movements**			
	At appropriate points in the lesson you moved about the teaching space	1 2 3	4	5 6 7
2.	**Teacher gestures**			
	You used gestures (hands, body, head, face) to convey extra meaning	1 2 3	4	5 6 7
3.	**Teacher voice**			
	You varied your rate, volume and expressiveness of speaking	1 2 3	4	5 6 7
4.	**Focusing**			
	Your important points were stressed by using gestures (pointing, etc.) or through words ('Watch this', 'Listen carefully', etc.)	1 2 3	4	5 6 7
5.	**Interactions**			
	You varied the kind of pupil participation (teacher-group; teacher-pupil; pupil-pupil)	1 2 3	4	5 6 7
6.	**Pausing**			
	You used pauses to give pupils time to think, to pay attention, to emphasize a point; that is, all teaching activity ceased for short periods	1 2 3	4	5 6 7
7.	**Oral-visual switching**			
	You used visual material in such a way that the pupils must look to get this information, not listen	1 2 3	4	5 6 7

Skill comments:

Explanation

The question 'What is an explanation?' has bedevilled philosophers for centuries (see Kahl, 1963). A detailed analysis of explaining, understanding and meaning would take us too far from the main task of helping you to give simple, clear, effective explanations. But it is as well to bear in mind that what may be a good explanation to one group of people may not be a good explanation to another group. In other words good explanations are a function of the skills, interests and capabilities of the class as well as being a function of the teacher's skills and knowledge. To explain is to give understanding to another.

ON GIVING EXPLANATIONS

Good explanations are like this author's favourite swimsuits: brief, appealing yet covering the essential features. One needs to distinguish between the lead-in to an explanation and the explanation itself. Lead-ins may be questions and answer sessions, discussions, demonstrations or brief lectures. They should attract attention and contribute to the structuring of the explanation. You must choose an appropriate lead-in for the group you are teaching. The explanation itself should be concise – lengthy qualifications and elaborations should follow the explanation not precede it. At the end of an explanatory sequence the main points should be summarized.

Now look back at the first paragraph of this section of explanation. Which sentence contains the heart of the explanation of the term 'explanation'? Does it match the criteria given in the second paragraph? What is the lead-in sentence in the second paragraph?

BREVITY

Brevity in the actual explanation is important so that the listener can easily recall and understand it. The audience research of the British Broadcasting Corporation indicates that talks that are too long or rambling are not easily recalled or understood by their audience. Ten minutes is the most suitable length for a radio talk involving an explanation. The core of the explanation may only take one minute or less. This does not mean that lectures should be abandoned and all classroom periods reduced to ten minutes. There is much more involved in teaching than merely giving explanations. But it does mean that teachers and lecturers do need to plan their lessons carefully so that their explanations are clear and presented in an interesting way. Hence the importance of all the skills of exposition and of listening, observing and responding to one's pupils during teaching. Often the pupils' non-verbal cues are a clear signal of their interest, concern or boredom. Skill in interpreting these cues is an important part of teaching (see p. 120).

Good explanations appeal to the listener – whether the listener is a pupil, a judge in a High Court or a man in the street. Simple illustrations, examples and analogies help to make explanation appealing. These principles have been used in this unit in the hope that you will enjoy reading and learning about teaching skills – and so learn about them more effectively.

The guidelines for using analogies, illustrations and examples are easy: make them interesting, simple and relevant.

COVERING THE ESSENTIAL FEATURES

The training you may have received in conceptual analysis (in a philosophy of education course) and the introduction to concept teaching (Unit II, pp. 42–46) are relevant to this discussion. To cover the essential features it is necessary to know *what they are* – so you can separate the items that the pupils need to know from those which it would be nice for them to know. You can then incorporate the essential features in your explanation. Which sentence in the previous sections contain the essential features of an explanation. Which sentence in the previous sections contain the essential features of appeal? (For further discussion and research on explanations see Thyne, 1963 and Gage, 1972).

Listening

So far we have outlined the characteristics of good explanations given by teachers. Teachers also listen to pupils' explanations. It is tempting to suggest that good teachers listen carefully and use the pupils' own ideas and words in giving their explanations. Excellent teachers train their pupils to give good explanations (see Unit VI, pp. 116–18). To achieve any of these goals it is necessary to learn how to listen effectively (Nichols, 1957 and Flanders, 1973).

Below are listed hints which will help you to listen effectively. They are also a useful guide to your own explanatory skills.

ORGANIZE

As the person talks, ask yourself:

1. What are the *main* points he is making?
2. What *supporting* facts or reasons does he give?
3. What *advantage* does he claim?
4. What *disadvantage* does he mention?

You can answer these questions in your mind whilst he is talking, or write down your answers during or immediately after he stops talking. You can do this by noting down the *key* words or phrases that he uses.

Bear in mind that most answers contain *relevant* and *irrelevant* information. As the person talks, sort out the relevant from the irrelevant, ignore the irrelevancies in your summary.

SUMMARIZE

Produce an oral or written summary of the main points.

BEWARE OF DISTRACTIONS

Most classrooms are noisy, active places. If the noise is too great, quieten the class, move closer to the pupil(s) and delay the discussion until it can easily be heard. Sometimes the distraction is due to differences in accent and dialect of the speakers, or their disorganized way of speaking. You must study the accents and dialects of your pupils so that you become familiar with them, and you must help pupils who are disorganized in their speech. A simple strategy which helps disorganized pupils is to praise them by saying: 'That's good, you've got all the points in your answer. Let's write them down and see if we can place them in a better order.'

After establishing a better order, ask them to give an improved explanation. Praise them again and suggest that they try next time to produce the points in order. Get their agreement to do this. The next time they offer an answer, encourage them if they try. If they have forgotten remind them that they agreed to try.

These simple guidelines will help you to be an effective listener to pupils, your own teachers, salesmen, political leaders and your friends. Much of the art of communicating is concerned with effective listening.

Activity 26

Choose a topic from a subject you are *NOT* studying at college, which is a little difficult for you to understand and which is suitable for use in a ten minute microlesson.

Read up the topic carefully. Extract the main points and summarize them.

Use the summary for the basis of a lesson plan. Plan your lesson carefully paying particular attention to your lead-in, the examples and illustrations you use and the explanation you give. Aim at summarizing your explanation at the end of the microlesson.

Teach the lesson and evaluate it on the schedule given on the next page. Write a brief paragraph indicating how you could improve upon the clarity and precision of your explanation.

TEACHER EXPLANATION APPRAISAL GUIDE

Teach/reteach (ring appropriate word)

Name: Topic: Class:

Date: Microteaching supervisor:

Please read the guide before you teach the microlesson, and
look through it whilst you are viewing the teaching session.

Assess your microteaching performance on each of the items rigorously,
as if you wer about to qualify as a teacher. Put a ring round the
number which most closely indicates your view of your performance.

7 represents 'truly outstanding' (for a person about to qualify)
and 1 represents 'weak'.

	Explanations	NO		YES
1.	Your explanations were clearly understood by the pupils	1 2 3	4	5 6 7
2.	Your explanations appealed to the pupils	·1 2 3	4	5 6 7
3.	Your explanations covered the essential features	1 2 3	4	5 6 7
4.	The analogies, illustrations and examples you used were interesting to the pupils	1 2 3	4	5 6 7
5.	The analogies, illustrations and examples you used were relevant to your explanations	1 2 3	4	5 6 7
6.	You listened carefully to the pupils' responses	1 2 3	4	5 6 7
7.	You clarified their responses, so helping the pupils to gain greater understanding	1 2 3	4	5 6 7

Skill comments:

Overview

This unit has introduced you to the skills of exposition and listening. You have carried out activities designed to help you to improve the ways you begin and end a lesson, to teach in a more lively, enthusiastic way and to explain ideas more lucidly and concisely. You will probably have discovered that gaining and holding the attention of pupils is not an easy task and that listening is by no means a passive process. You should now reread this unit and tackle the next activity which requires you to practise and analyse all the teaching skills of this unit.

Activity 27

Choose a topic which will be of interest to your pupils. Plan and teach a ten minute microlesson based upon it. Pay particular attention to how you introduce the topic, your liveliness within the lesson, the quality of your explanations and the way you close the lesson.

Rate your performance on the Classroom Guidance Schedule and analyse the lesson using BIAS. (Look particularly at the occurrences of silence.)

Write a paragraph summarizing the improvements you need to make to your exposition skills.

Unit VI · Questioning and answering

This unit has been designed to improve your skills in questioning and to help you to improve your pupils' skills in answering. On completing the unit you should be able to:

    (i) Identify various types of question;
    (ii) Effectively use the various types of questions in your teaching;
    (iii) Help your pupils to give better answers.

Your awareness of the various types of questions will also help you to plan ways of monitoring and evaluating the pupils' learning.

Questioning

The skills of questioning are as old as instruction itself. They are the basis of the method of teaching developed by Socrates in the fifth century B.C., they were used extensively by the schoolmen of the Middle Ages and today they are used by almost every teacher in every classroom. Despite this long history of the use of questions, it is surprisingly difficult to define precisely what constitutes a question. A rough and ready description would be 'any statement which tests or creates knowledge in the learner'. Such a definition excludes *compliance* and *rhetorical* questions such as the teacher saying 'Will you please stop talking' or 'Well, what are the main points about the pass laws?' followed by the teacher answering the question himself. The first directs the pupils to be silent. The second requires no answer by the pupils. They are expected to sit and passively listen. This operational definition of a question also highlights two major kinds of questions (see particularly p. 107 et. seq.). Questions which test knowledge may be described as *lower order cognitive questions*. For example, What is the capital of France? There are usually correct single answers to these types of questions. Questions which create new knowledge in the learner may be referred to as *higher order cognitive questions*. There are usually no correct answers to these questions – although some answers are clearly better than others. Further details of these types of questions are given in various sections below.

    The long history of the use of questions contains a further suprise: most teachers rarely use higher order questions. Yet it is precisely these questions which stimulate man's highest levels of thinking. In a review by Gall (1970) it is estimated that over 60 per cent of all teachers' questions require students to recall facts, 20 per cent of teachers' questions require students to think and 20 per cent are concerned with procedural matters (such as, 'Have you finished writing yet?'). These are average figures for all teachers surveyed in the United States and one can safely conclude that many teachers' questions never soar above the recall of an idea. About one third of teacher talk is questioning and, on average, each teacher asks about two questions per minute. Higher rates are recorded in elementary schools than in secondary schools. The evidence reviewed by Rosenshine (1971) shows that frequency of questions bears no relationship to the level of pupil achievement in tests and examinations and that higher level questioning is positively related to higher level performance in tests and examinations. Obviously if the tests or examinations require only low level answers, as in simple arithmetic, then low level questions in class are likely to be as effective as more sophisticated questions. This is also borne out by Rosenshine's evidence. The conclusion which can be drawn from this evidence is that one has to consciously choose what kinds of learning one wants to promote. Then one should choose the appropriate levels of questions.

It is not enough, however, to choose the appropriate level of questions. One must also know how to communicate that question effectively to a group of pupils.

Increasing fluency in asking questions

Ultimately, questions are only as good as the answers that they evoke. This section of the unit has been designed to improve your general questioning techniques. The hints and suggestions that follow are of value in all discussion sessions – regardless of the types of questions you are using. For convenience, I have isolated eight elements in fluency which you study and then practise in Activity 28. The eight elements are clarity and coherence, pausing and pacing, directing and distributing, and, prompting and probing.

Clarity and coherence

Below are three questions. Read them and rank them in terms of their clarity and coherence.

> (i) Well, er, that's um er very interesting and what er I think I ought to um er do now is ask someone, or one of you whether you would er prefer to fish in the Bann with a rod or a harpoon gun.
> (ii) Paul. Which do you think is better for fishing in the Bann, a rod or a harpoon gun?
> (iii) Peter. Do you think you would fish with a rod in the Bann or would you buy a harpoon?

Most of you will have put (i) lowest on your list for the question is unclear and incoherent. Indeed it is hard to tell that it is a question. The question is obscured by the 'ums' and ers'. It is also not clear that it is a question until the teacher stops speaking. The second example is clear and coherent. It is brief, to the point and directed at a specific person in the class. The third example is brief and incoherent. For it offers the pupil two conflicting alternatives. Peter may want to fish with a rod *and* buy a harpoon gun. Such a question would confuse most pupils. We call questions with conflicting alternatives 'double barrelled questions'. One should avoid shooting them at pupils – unless your intention is to deliberately confuse them.

Clear and coherent questions need to be planned. This is particularly important when you are using high level cognitive questions. In the early stages of teaching such questions should be written down in the lesson plans and scrutinized carefully. What may be a clear and coherent question to someone steeped in a subject may be conceptually muddy to a secondary school pupil. Occasionally rephrasing a question in the lesson can help, but in the early stages of teaching you should avoid rephrasing questions as much as possible. Very often initial attempts at rephrasing confuse the pupils instead of helping them to understand the question.

Pausing and pacing

Beginner teachers frequently ask more questions than they receive answers (Brown, 1973; Macbeth, 1972; Wragg, 1972). Their failure to obtain answers is often due to lack of pauses and no variation in their delivery of questions (pacing). Immediately after asking a question you should pause and look around the class. There are non-verbal cues which tell you whether someone has the answer. The raising of a hand is the formal signal that a pupil is ready to respond, but before this occurs there are other signals to look for. When a person is ready to answer he opens his mouth slightly, he may lean forward slightly, he may open his eyes slightly wider or he may raise his head. Be on the look out for these signals during the pause after asking a question. The length of pause also acts as a signalling device to pupils. A short pause before repeating or rephrasing the question indicates you are expecting prompt answers. A long pause (over three seconds) indicates you are expecting pupils to think carefully before answering the question. Which sort of pause would you use after a low level cognitive question?

The speed of delivery of a question is determined partly by the kind of question being asked. Low level drill questions can be asked quickly, more complex questions should be preceded by a short pause, asked slowly and clearly, and followed by a long pause. Asking complex questions at the quicker pace results in confusion and the pupils will probably remain silent and bewildered.

When you first start using pausing and pacing behaviour you should help the pupils to learn what you want them to do. Immediately follow a high level question by remarks such as 'Now, think over your answer carefully' or 'Please try to give a full answer.' *Then* pause for three or more seconds. When you are going to use quick fire questioning techniques you should first say 'Now I'm going to ask you some questions and I want you to answer them as quickly as you can.' Start firing the questions and pause only briefly before calling upon a pupil to answer. These remarks can gradually be dropped and eventually your pausing and pacing will become the signals for the kinds of answers being sought.

Directing and distributing

Some pupils are more willing to answer questions in class than others. These pupils are often brighter and more attractive. They usually know the answers that the teacher is seeking. The teacher finds such pupils rewarding and he may, therefore, unwittingly devote more time to these pupils than to their less forthcoming peers. In this way the teacher unintentionally produces a cleavage in the class between a small group of active participants and a large group of passive learners. Their passivitiy may change to boredom, then to deviant behaviour and discipline problems for the teacher. These problems can be minimized by directing questions to specific pupils and distributing the questions around the class. Whilst asking questions one should monitor the class to see who is and is not attending. A question directed at someone who is not attending-can be a useful controlling device. One should pay particular attention to children sitting near the back and at the side of a formal classroom. These are areas which many teachers neglect (Adams and Biddle, 1970).

If a question cannot be answered by the first person asked, you can, after a pause, redirect it to another pupil or set of pupils. This keeps the pupils alert and more ready to learn.

Perhaps the most common weakness of beginners is to not control pupils' answers. You should always direct your attention at a specific person when you ask a question by using the name of a pupil, e.g. 'Christine, do you . . .', rather than 'Do you . . .', or by looking pointedly at one pupil. The pupil you look at need not be the one you want to answer the question. Do not accept answers that are called out. This leads to problems of control and ineffective teaching. If several pupils shout answers, the temptation is to pick the right answer out of the chorus. This reinforces the shouting of the pupils and so encourages them to shout again. It does not allow a teacher to reward the individual who gave the correct (or interesting) answer, nor does it allow the probing of a wrong answer. Shouting by pupils increases the volume of noise, heightens the problems of control and reduces the quality of teaching.

So far, directing and distributing have been discussed in terms of minimizing discipline problems. Skilful directing and distributing also involves pupils more closely. They are more likely to participate and enjoy discussions if they know that they have a fair share of discussion time. There are, however, always some pupils who are reluctant to participate in discussion. Directing questions in a non-threatening way towards such pupils will help to draw them into the discussion. If they respond then their response should as far as possible be praised and subsequently used again in the discussion. If they cannot respond, one should redirect the question to another pupil after giving them an encouraging nod and remark. *What would you do if a very shy child did answer but his answer was completely wrong?* (See page 147.)

Prompting and probing

TEACHER. Would you say that nationalism in Africa is now greater than it was twenty years ago?

PUPIL. Greater.

TEACHER. Yes. Why is that?

PUPIL. Because there are more nations now.

TEACHER. Yes. Mmm. There's more to it than that. Can anyone else give some reasons?

CLASS. (Silence).

TEACHER. Well, basically it's because . . .

This is an example of what frequently happens in the first discussion lessons given by a teacher. The discussion drags and degenerates into an unprepared lecture. This can be avoided by prompting or probing any weak answers given.

Prompting consists of giving hints to help the pupil. In the example just given the teacher could have said 'Yes. That's right. There are more nations now and there are more nations because African people wanted to be independent of the Europeans. What has happened in the past twenty years which has helped them to become independent?' A series of prompts, followed by encouragement, can help pupils to gain confidence in giving replies.

Probing questions direct the pupil to think more deeply about his initial answer and to express himself more clearly. In so doing they develop a pupil's critical awareness and his communication skills.

TEACHER Jessica. You went to Paris this year. What did you think of it?

JESSICA Mmm. It was nice.

TEACHER What was nice about it? (Pause)

JESSICA Well, I liked walking down the avenues which had trees. I liked watching the boats on the river. I liked listening to Frenchmen. The Metro was exciting and, oh, I liked the French bread and butter.

The simple probe 'What was nice about it?' evoked from this seven-year-old girl a series of impressions which revealed her interests in sights, sounds and food. Probing questions with older and more sophisticated children tap the highest levels of their thinking. You may be agreeably surprised by what such questions can reveal.

[108]

Activity 28

1. Read the previous sections of this unit, the section on 'Listening' in the previous unit (pp. 99–100) and the rating schedule which follows.
2. Plan a microlesson of ten minutes' duration which involves questions and answers. In your lesson plan give examples of the sorts of questions you hope to ask, and a summary of the points you expect the question and answer lesson to cover.
3. Teach the lesson. Pay particular attention to the items described on the rating schedule which follows. Ensure that you summarize the main points of the question and answer session in your closure of the lesson.
4. Use the BIAS (with the p extension, p. 75ff) and estimate the number of questions and replies given. Exclude rhetorical and compliance questions — they are not TQs in the BIAS system. Count rephrased questions as if they were new questions. Check the lesson on the 'Fluency in Asking Questions' guide. Discuss ways in which your fluency in questioning might be improved and then write a brief paragraph in which you summarize the suggested improvements.

Categories of teacher questions

Lower	1. Compliance	The pupil is expected to comply with a command worded as a question.
	2. Rhetorical	The pupil is not expected to reply. The teacher answers his own question.
	3. Recall	Does the pupil recall what he has seen or read?
	4. Comprehension	Does the pupil understand what he recalls?
	5. Application	Can the pupil apply rules and techniques to solve problems that have single correct answers?
Higher	6. Analysis	Can the pupil identify motives and causes, make inferences and give examples to support his statements?
	7. Synthesis	Can the pupil make predictions, solve problems or produce interesting juxtapositions of ideas and images?
	8. Evaluation	Can the pupil judge the quality of ideas, or problem solutions, or works of art? Can he give rationally based opinions on issues or controversies?

Levels of questions

I said in the introduction to this unit that one can distinguish questions which test knowledge and questions which create knowledge. The former are called lower order cognitive questions and the latter are referred to as higher order cognitive questions. The chart below sets out the classification of questions adopted from Bloom's (1956) taxonomy of the cognitive domain.

FLUENCY IN ASKING QUESTIONS

Read this schedule before planning and teaching your microlesson on questioning and immediately before viewing your lesson.

Ring the appropriate word

1. Your questions were usually clearly understood by the pupils — Yes   No

2. Your questions were usually coherently expressed — Yes   No

3. You used pauses after askjng most of your questions — Yes   No

4. You varied the pace at which you asked questions — Yes   No

5. You directed some of your questions at individual pupils — Yes   No

6. You distributed your questions amongst the whole group of pupils — Yes   No

7. You used prompting techniques to help pupils formulate their answers — Yes   No

8. You used probing techniques to help pupils think more deeply about their answers — Yes   No

Skill comments:

You will have noticed that the categories of questions are described in terms of the pupils's expected responses. This is to remind you to check that your questions evoke the type of answer intended. A grunt from a pupil as an answer to the question 'What do you think Europe will be like in ten years' time?' cannot be regarded as a successful question.

How would you classify the question on Europe's future? (See page 147 for answer.)

Lower order cognitive questions

Recall

Recall questions may be split into two types:

a. Those requiring a Yes or No. These are labelled binary questions.
b. Those requiring the recall of a word, phrase or series of sentences. These may be labelled recall questions. The recall need not be literal.

Binary questions rarely give opportunities for thinking deeply and they allow a 50 per cent chance of guessing correctly. If the pupil is good at spotting the teacher's non-verbal cues, his chances are even greater. A typical binary question is 'Is London the capital of England?' Sometimes there are variations on this to try to catch the pupils out. 'Paris *is* the capital of Germany, isn't it?' This may be handled in a friendly, humorous way or in a malicious, sadistic way. The latter is questionable.

Recall questions range from the one word answer – 'What is the capital of Iran?' to questions involving the recall of linked ideas – 'Can you remember how the steam engine works?' Recall questions at this level shade off into the higher order questions of comprehension.

Many teachers confine their questions to this level of recall virtually all the time. Hence the opportunity for pupil participation and independent thinking in many classes is rare. This does not mean that recall questions should not be asked. It does mean that they should be used sparingly, that you should be aware when you are using them, and that preferably you should use them only in the early stages of a discussion.

Comprehension

Three categories of comprehension questions may be distinguished:

a. Giving a description in one's own words.
    Example: 'Could you describe what happened in your last microteaching lesson?'
b. Stating the main ideas in one's own words.
    Example: 'Could you state the main characteristics of remembering and comprehension questions?'

c. Comparing.

Example: 'What are the similarities and differences between remembering and comprehension questions?'

Generally speaking comprehension questions refer only to information and skills learnt in recent lessons. They simply *test* whether the pupil has understood what he has been learning. Where the student must work out the answer for himself the question becomes an analysis question.

Application

Application questions set up a simple problem situation which the pupil has to solve with his recently acquired or recalled knowledge. Many mathematics and science questions are of this type. A pupil may have learnt to solve the equations: $x + 4 = 10$ and $2x = 22$. The next question might ask him to apply the principles he has learnt to solve the equation $2x + 4 = 32$.

In other subjects application questions are most frequently used to encourage pupils to correctly distinguish different categories of events, images and ideas. For example, you may have taught a class the key characteristics of sonnets. You might then present them with a fourteen-line poem written in blank verse and ask them to apply their knowledge to decide whether the poem is in fact a sonnet. Application questions are used in concept teaching (see Unit II).

Higher order cognitive questions

Analysis

Analysis questions require a pupil to identify motives and causes or make deductions or inductions. Like all higher order questions, they have no single correct answer and the answers cannot be obtained by merely reading or remembering instructional materials. Nonetheless one has to be wary of too crisp or succinct answers from pupils. They may be recalling part of a text or crammer's books on the topic and not thinking at a higher level.

Below are a few examples of analysis questions in various subjects:

Why did Huck Finn decide not to report Jim as a runaway slave?
Why do the Eskimoes have so many words for snow?
What makes you think it is very hot in Siberia in summer?
What can one conclude about Ibo family life?
What does this tell us about the author's feelings for children?
What evidence do we have that ice is lighter than water?

Such questions require pupils to organize their thoughts, to look for evidence, to interpret or make generalizations. This is high level thinking and you must not expect your pupils to achieve this without help and encouragement. Pupils often give brief or incomplete answers to analysis questions so one has to prompt and probe.

Activity 29

1. Reread the previous section of the unit.
2. Read the extract from a tapescript of a lesson given below.
3. Classify the questions as R (Recall), C (Comprehension), Ap (Application), or U (Unclassified). Write the appropriate letter in the right hand margin.
4. Count the number of cognitive questions in the extract.

TEACHER. Good morning, boys and girls. Peter, could you please open the window?   a ....
No one knows what we're going to do today, do they?   b ....
Well, I'll tell you. We are going to see what we can remember about capital cities. Ben, what is the capital of France?
PUPIL. Paris.
TEACHER. Yes. That's right. Jessica. What is the capital of England?   d ....
PUPIL. London.
TEACHER. And Jenny. What is the capital of Austria?   e ....
PUPIL. Vienna
TEACHER. Very good. Now can someone tell me what these cities have in common? (Pause)   f ....
PUPIL. Well they're all capital cities and they are all big cities.
TEACHER. That's very good, John. Sheila, can you add anything to that? (Pause)   g ....
PUPIL. (Silent, no reply)
TEACHER. Well, what makes a city into a capital?   h ....
PUPIL. Oh, it's where the king lives and where all the government is.
TEACHER. Splendid, Sheila! Now what do Paris, London and Vienna have which helped them to be important? (Pause)   i ....
Something which was very useful in days when there was no aeroplane and the roads were bad. (Pause)   j ....
PUPIL. Oh, of course! They all had big rivers going through them, so they could use boats.
TEACHER. That's right! London, Paris and Vienna first became important because they had rivers which carried trade   k ....

See page 147 for answers to 3 and 4.

Synthesis

Synthesis may be split into two types:

a. Questions that ask pupils to make predictions.
Examples: What would happen to this tree if Peter poured acid on its roots? What do you think your life will be like in ten years' time?

b. Questions that require pupils to sensitively express ideas and images.
    Examples: What must it be like to be blind? Think about all the things you would miss if you were blind.
    Imagine you are a young African living in a village in the bush 200 years ago. Suddenly two men with white skins appear. They are carrying strange weapons. What would be your reaction?

Synthesis questions stimulate the pupils' creative potential. The answer to such questions requires time for reflection. They are most suitable for written assignments and lessons devoted entirely to discussion. Nonetheless, with a little ingenuity and synthesis one can invent interesting questions for microteaching. For example, the question 'What must it be like to be blind?' can be used in a microlesson on creative writing.

The teacher needs to gain the attention of the class and then quietly say 'What must it be like to be blind? Close your eyes gently and think of all the things you would miss seeing, think of all the people you would miss seeing, their faces, their smile, their hands. Think of all the things and people you would miss seeing. Move your hands gently along the desk top. Can you feel its rough edges? Stroke the paper of your books. Now stroke the desk. Do you notice the differences? Now listen to the sounds around you. (Pause) You would notice sounds and the feel of things more if you were blind. But what would you miss most? Think about it. In a few moments time, I shall ask you to open your eyes and write down whatever comes into your head about being blind. It doesn't matter about the spelling and grammar – just write what you think. Think what it would be like never to see again. What would you miss most?' (Half-minute silence) 'Now open your eyes quickly and write it down.'

This type of introduction usually stimulates even quite unoriginal pupils to write creatively. What they write may then need structuring or putting in blank verse form. This, too, should be done gently and sensitively.

In answering synthesis questions, a pupil creates or discovers ideas which are new to him and uses these in giving his answer.

Here is a list of common openings in synthesis questions.

Can you think up . . . (a title for a story)?
What would it be like . . . (to be an old man with no friends)?
How can we solve . . . (the problem of infant mortality in poor countries)?
How can we improve . . . (general understanding of a government's policies)?
What will happen . . . (to books now we have television)?
What do you think would happen if . . . (the ice on the North Pole melted)?

Evaluation

It can be argued that evaluation questions are the highest forms of thinking we attain. No matter how brilliant a synthesis answer is, we must evaluate it, we must reckon its worth. When John Dewey observed that 'to think is to question' he had in mind this type of question. Any civilization concerned with change and improvement must

Activity 30

Reread the previous sections of this unit. Write a higher order question on the same topics as given in the lower order questions set out below. Try to use as many of the three kinds of higher order questions as you can. Indicate in parentheses which type of question you have created.

Example:
Lower order question: What were the years of the Vietnam war?
Higher order question: Why was there a war in Vietnam? (**Evaluation**)
What caused the recent Vietnam war? (**Analysis**)
What might have been the sufferings of a young Vietnamese girl in the recent war? (**Synthesis**)
Write your answer as a short story.
In the example three alternatives are given. In the activity you are asked to give only one.

1. What is the largest city in Holland?
2. Who is the author of *Catcher in the Rye*?
3. What does the theorem of Pythagoras tell us?
4. Who wrote Hamlet?
5. What happened in *A Christmas Carol*?
6. What is the most common element found in the earth's crust?
7. What is the most widely spoken indigenous language in Africa?
8. Where is Stonehenge?
9. How many independent countries have been established in Africa during the past twenty years?
10. What are the two main levels of questions?

Some suggestions will be found on p. 148.

foster this form of questioning. It encourages pupils to discriminate between different ideas and values, and works of art, and it encourages them to give reasons for their judgements. In so doing it makes explicit their reasons so that they are more open to change along rational lines.

We can distinguish four main categories of evaluation questions:

a. Questions that require pupils to give their opinions about issues.
Example : Do you think women teachers should wear mini-skirts in school?
b. Questions that require pupils to judge the values of ideas.
Example: Do you think it is true that Marx's ideas have had more influence than Jesus Christ's?

Activity 31

1. Plan a microlesson of ten minutes' duration on a discussion topic which will be of interest to the group of pupils that you are teaching.
2. Write out five higher order questions which you are going to try to use in the lesson.
3. Write out two possible answers which members of the group might give to each of the questions.
4. Give an example of a prompt and a probe for each of your questions.
5. Teach the lesson. Ensure you summarize the main points of discussion at the end of the lesson.
6. View and analyse the lesson with a friend.
    a. Rate your lesson on the 'Fluency in Asking Questions' guide.
    b. Re-view the lesson and analyse it using the BIAS technique described in Unit IV. Use the extension for higher and lower order questions (I, h). Estimate the number of questions asked, the number of responses. Compare the length of answers after the lower and higher order questions. Examine the occurrences of silence on the display.
    c. Discuss your use of lower and higher order questions.
    d. Write a paragraph summarizing the suggestions to improve your techniques.

c. Questions that require pupils to judge the merits of various solutions to problems.
    Example : Which seems to be the best method of drilling oil in Nigeria?
d. Questions that require pupils to judge the merits of works of art.
    Example : Why do you think folk music is better than classical music?

As in all higher cognitive questions the initial questions may not achieve a high quality answer. Hence one must probe by asking Why? Are there any other reasons? What does anyone else think? In this way you can help pupils become aware of the complexity of some questions and that there are many ways of looking at a problem. This will help them to consider many different viewpoints and arrive at more balanced and rational opinions.

Here is a list of common openings to evaluation questions.

Do you agree . . . ? Why?   Which is best . . . ? Why?
Do you think . . . ? Why?   Which do you like . . . ? Why?
What is your opinion . . . ? Why? Do you believe . . . ? Why?
Would it be better . . . ? Why?   Do you consider . . . ? Why?

Helping pupils to improve their answers

Just as there are skills involved in asking questions so there are skills in giving answers. The quality of a discussion lesson can be improved by teaching pupils about lower order and higher order questions, and by helping them to comment on each others' (and their own) answers.

I suggest you use the terms 'fact' and 'thought' questions when you are teaching the pupils about questions. A useful approach is to write on the blackboard or overhead projector two lists of questions. One list should contain only simple 'fact' questions, the other should consist of only 'thought' questions. Ask the pupils to look at the lists and to work out what the difference is between them. Then ask them which kind of questions they prefer and why. You will probably need to use directing and redirecting, prompts and probes to obtain answers to this question. You should then set a simple exercise consisting of a list of ten simple 'fact' and 'thought' questions. The pupils should be asked to decide which are 'fact' and which are 'thought' questions. You should end the lesson by explaining that knowing what kinds of questions are being asked will help them to give better answers in class and in their homework.

Teaching pupils to evaluate each others' answers requires sensitive skill. Blundering can shatter some pupils' confidence in giving answers. It is therefore suggested that you:

1. Set a simple exercise on a topic requiring pupils to give their opinions. Example: Write a short answer (not more than five lines) on Why do children go to school?

2. Before the pupils hand in the exercise: Put up on the blackboard or overhead projector three or four answers of differing quality. Ask the pupils to read the answers and to try to decide which is best, and why. Develop a discussion on this theme. You will probably have to use all the fluency skills I have described earlier in this unit. Summarize the main points of what constitute good answers to the question 'Why do children go to school?' (or your chosen topic).

3. Ask the pupils to amend their answers in the light of the discussion (this could be their next homework exercise), and to answer another simple thought question.

4. Mark their answers carefully. Praise their good points and suggest ways of improving upon their answers.
   Note: This is, of course, how one should always mark pupils' work.

Set out below is a checklist of what constitutes a good answer to a question. It will help you and your pupils to give better answers. Read the checklist, work out how you will explain it to your pupils and go through it carefully with them.

1. Is my answer **clear**?
    Am I using understandable English in my answers and not confusing the person who is listening to me, or reading my answer?
2. Is my answer **accurate**?
    Have I given facts and figures which are not true?
3. Is my answer **appropriate**?
    Have I answered the questions which I was asked?
4. Is my answer **specific**?
    Will the teacher or the person reading or listening to my answer know who and what I am writing or talking about?·
5. Does my answer contain **support** for my views?
    Have I given reasons, fact, or examples to support my argument or opinions?
6. Does my answer show an awareness of **complexity**?
    Have I looked at more than one side of the question?

Activity 32

1. Reread the previous section.
2. Plan three linked microlessons, each of ten minutes' duration, designed to improve the quality of pupils' answers in an area of your teaching subject. Include in your plan of the first lesson a follow-up exercise for the pupils which they should complete in the interval between the first and second lessons. Include in your plan of the second lesson a follow-up exercise for the pupils which they should complete in the interval between the second and third lessons.
3. View your lessons and rate them on the 'Fluency in Asking Questions' guide.
4. Mark the pupils' written exercises constructively. Show them to a friend and discuss with him whether he agrees with the suggestions and comments you have written on each pupils' answer. Return the marked answers to the pupils.

Note: This exercise is best carried out with secondary school pupils. If you are microteaching with peers it is suggested that only two of the group should actually microteach their lessons. The lesson plans of the remaining students should be discussed and improved upon by the team of peers.

The procedures I have suggested will help in the initial stages of aiding your pupils to think, rather than to recall. Many pupils are not used to thinking or, rather, to revealing their thinking to their teachers. Hence you should not expect to be entirely successful in the early stages. Nonetheless adopting the procedures suggested will help your pupils, regardless of their ability, to develop their own thinking and communication skills. I suggest that when you begin teaching you should periodically check the categories of questions you are asking in class. The following activities will help you and your pupils to maintain higher levels of thinking.

1. Include some higher cognitive questions in tests and written assignments.
2. Continue to draw the attention of your pupils to good answers – and discuss why they are good.
3. Make a videotape or audiotape of an occasional discussion lesson and analyse it. Use BIAS and estimate the number of lower and higher order questions you use. Check your fluency on the 'Fluency in Asking Questions' guide.

Finally, a question: *Why should a teacher use some higher order questions?* (Answer, p. 148.)

Overview

This unit has been concerned with improving questioning and answering. You have been introduced to tactics which will make your questions more fluent, you have been shown and given practice in the use and analysis of various categories of questions and some ways of improving your pupils' answers have been suggested. Of the skills described in this unit I would single out prompting, probing and higher order questioning as ones which require continued and intensive practice. You should also pay particular attention to the skills of listening and summarizing which were outlined in the previous unit. The next unit focuses on ways of increasing pupil participation. When you have studied and practised the skills described in the next unit you will have acquired a complete repertoire of discussion skills which you will find useful not only in the classroom but also in staff meetings and committees.

Unit VII · Participation in discussion

Introduction

Discussion may be regarded as conversations with a purpose. Their purpose in teaching is to promote interest and learning. The task of a discussion leader involves explaining, listening, questioning, clarifying answers, encouraging participants, controlling the discussions, using the ideas of the group and summarizing their views. Exposition and listening skills were outlined in Unit V and questioning and answering in Unit VI. This unit focuses upon the skills of participation. The first section of the unit is designed to sharpen your perception of the attending behaviours of pupils. This is a preliminary to learning how to use the reinforcement techniques which are covered in the second section. Unless you know whether your pupils are attending then you cannot begin to influence their behaviour. The reinforcement techniques in their turn serve as a preliminary to the core skills of using the pupils' own ideas and varying interactions. Unless you know how to praise and control your pupils you are unlikely to be able to use their ideas in discussion. On completing the unit you should be able to :

1. Identify the main characteristics of attending behaviours.
2. Use a wide range of reinforcement techniques.
3. Gain and control pupil participation in discussion activities.

Attending to pupil behaviours

Try this test of your perception.
1. Imagine a teacher talking to a class in a dull, monotonous voice. As he talks he looks at the floor and occasionally shuffles his feet. The class are bored and listless. Close your eyes and try to picture how the class are sitting, their body positions and their facial expressions. Write down a brief description of the bored class.
2. Now imagine another teacher with the same class of children. The teacher is standing by the blackboard. He occasionally writes on the blackboard. The class is very interested in what is going on. Close your eyes and picture how this class is sitting, the body positions and facial expressions of the pupils. Write down a brief description of the interested class.

Carry out the above task before reading on.

Bored pupils usually slouch and turn slightly away from the teacher. They rest their chins on their hands and often try to hide their faces. Their faces are expressionless and unsmiling. Their eyelids may be partially closed and their mouths turned down.

A few pupils may be doodling or combing their fingers through their hair. Occasionally in a very bored class a pupil will involuntarily drop his head. He is nodding off.

Lively interested classes usually sit with their heads slightly forward, their eyes are open wide and a few of them will be restlessly waiting for a chance to speak. Almost all of them will be turned towards the teacher. A few in a discussion lesson may be unofficially communicating with each other by using head nods and whispers.

The brief description in the previous paragraph does not cover all the pupils' signals of boredom or interest but it is sufficient to give you the 'feel' of bored and interested classes. Time lapse photography of classes has increased our knowledge of the signals of boredom and interest. In some studies these signals have been related to pupil achievement and attitudes and in others time lapse has been used to develop teachers' perceptions of attending behaviours (MacGraw, 1965; Fanslow, 1965; Grobe and Pettibone, 1973). All these studies stress the importance of attending behaviours as a necessary requisite of classroom learning.

You should monitor your classes most of the time you are teaching them. The feedback you receive will help you to anticipate when to switch activities, take a break or change to a different topic. Monitoring is an important element in classroom control. Some of you may have had a teacher who appeared to have eyes in the back of his head. He could tell when someone was not working when he was turned away from them and writing on the board. Such a teacher was using a simple trick. He had scanned the class just before he turned to the board so he knew who was not working but he did not say so until he was not looking at them (Kounin, 1970). You should also look for the pupils' signals of attention during discussions – especially if one pupil is dominating the discussion – and in audio-visual presentations. It is also important to monitor your pupils when you are lecturing to them or giving directions as in a laboratory class.

I have summarized below the main signals to look for when monitoring your classes. You should use the summary as a checklist when teaching the microlesson given in Activity 33.

Signals of pupils' attention
1. *Posture*: Are the pupils turned away from or towards the object of the lesson?
2. *Head orientation*: Are the pupils looking at or away from the object of the lesson? Are their heads up or down?
3. *Face*: Do the pupils look sleepy or awake? Do they look withdrawn or involved? Do they look uninterested or interested?
4. *Activities*: Are the pupils working on something related to the lesson? Are they furtively communicating with each other? Are they actively trying to communicate with you or their fellow pupils?
5. *Responses*: Are the pupils making inappropriate responses to your questions?

Activity 33

1. Plan a ten minute microteaching lesson which includes some lecturing and group discussion.
2. Turn the camera so that it videotapes the pupils. (Alternatively, if the camera is fixed, move the pupils so they are facing the camera.)
3. Teach your microlesson.
4. Read the 'signals of pupils' attention' given above.
5. View the videotape. Pay particular attention to the signals of pupil attention during the lecture segment and discussion segment. Use a stopwatch to find when the first signals of inattentiveness occurred and the time you recaptured the pupils' attention.
6. Discuss the videotape. Your discussion should focus upon the cues which pupils give when they are attending and not attending.
7. Write a brief description of the changes in attentiveness of the pupils and their relationship to the lesson activities.

Pupil reinforcement

Reinforcement is the technical term used to describe any technique which modifies or changes behaviour. Reinforcement may be positive (rewarding) or negative (witholding rewards, corrective feedback and punishment). The reinforcement may give the recipient information or feedback about his actions and thus act as a corrective to his behaviour. This section of the unit is concerned largely with positive reinforcement and corrective feedback. Punishment is not considered for it hardly ever produces long term changes in behaviour. Its main use is to temporarily suppress 'wrong behaviour'. Whilst the 'wrong' behaviour is being suppressed instruction on correct behaviour can be given and when the appropriate behaviour appears it should be rewarded. The technique of using reinforcement to change behaviour was largely developed by B. F. Skinner. In one of his famous lectures on reinforcement he described the principles of behaviour shaping whilst casually throwing corn to a hungry pigeon. By the end of the lecture he had usually convinced the audience of the effects of reinforcement and the pigeon of the necessity of executing a figure of eight before pecking corn.

The shaping of a pigeon's behaviour may seem remote from the behaviour of a human being. Yet despite our complexity we are susceptible to reinforcement and corrective feedback and use it every day of our lives. Here are a few examples:

(i) Your daughter unexpectedly wins a prize at school. You are delighted and say, 'My. Isn't that marvellous. You won!'

(ii) You are telling a friend about an incident. He leans forward and looks interested so you continue speaking.

(iii) An acquaintance rings you very late when you are in bed. He says he is sorry to disturb you. You reply in a frosty voice. 'It's quite all right.'

(iv) You are telling a friend about an incident. He leans back in his chair, yawns and looks at his watch. You ask him if he is interested and you cut your story short.

Reinforcement and feedback are the best tested principles in experimental psychology. Yet it is only in the past decade that serious attempts have been made to study them in the classroom. The evidence strongly indicates that various aspects of praise and corrective feedback are positively correlated with pupils' achievement and positive attitudes (Flanders and Simon, 1969; Rosenshine, 1971). A moment's reflection on your own experience as a pupil is likely to convince you of the importance of praise and help from a teacher. Praise and help not only change behaviour, they develop confidence and a positive self image. Their complete absence may lead to a poor self image and an unwillingness to keep trying. Not all pupils need sustained praise and help. A pupil who is clever and happy may not need positive reinforcement for each success. At the other extreme, a pupil who is weak academically and unhappy may need considerable help and praise, particularly during the early stages of learning a new task. Younger pupils seem to require more praise than older pupils and they are sensitive to the absence or withdrawal of praise. Often a child's inexplicable distress on arriving home from school may be tracked down to a tiny yet critical incident in which he was not praised or he was blamed by his teacher.

Three types of immediate reinforcers are available to the teacher — verbal, extra-verbal and non-verbal. He may also have sanctions and rewards — such as detaining a pupil after school or giving him high marks or a gold star. All this helps to give the teacher 'social power' over his pupils. The sanctions and rewards are part of the framework in which the teacher operates. The immediate reinforcers are what he must use most of the time. Frequent recourse to his sanctions and rewards weaken this framework and may result in a total collapse of his social power.

Controlling discussion through reinforcement

Praise encourages pupils to contribute to discussion as well as encouraging them to strive to achieve. The praise may be verbal such as 'That's splendid!' 'Very good!' 'Fantastic!' It may be non-verbal such as a smile, a nod of the head or friendly eye contact. It may be extra-verbal such as 'Mmmmm' or 'Aaaah!' Usually praise is a mixture of the three. Too frequent verbal praise results in loss of its rewarding properties. The pupils are likely to think you are not discriminating if you praise everything. Non-verbal praise is a discreet way of rewarding shy people who may be embarrassed by public praise. Extra-verbal praise is almost always used in conjunction with verbal and non-verbal praise.

Corrective feedback also keeps discussion going. It, too, may be verbal, extra-verbal or non-verbal. Corrective verbal feedback consists of prompts, probes and giving directions. All of these skills have been described in other units. Examples of appropriate corrective feedback statements and questions are:

> No, not quite. Try again.
> Could you say a bit more about it?
> Look at your book again and check your answer.
> Oh, you mean . . .?
> Could you give an example?

Extra-verbal feedback consists of Mmm's, Ah's and Ah ha's. This sort of feedback may be coupled with non-verbal cues such as a puzzled frown, raising the eybrows, frowning, scratching one's head, cocking one's head, looking at a pupil in a thoughtful way, pointing at a pupil, pointing from pupil to pupil or simply looking in silence. Silence is a particularly effective way of getting pupils to talk. As a matter of fact many pupils knowingly or unknowingly use silence to control their teachers. The teacher asks a question and the pupils remain silent. An inexperienced teacher will fill the silence by answering the question himself. What would an experienced teacher do? Finally, there is the 'stop' cue. The teacher can halt a wrong or irrelevant response by holding the arm straight with the hand up and palm out.

Using reinforcement in other teaching situations

A teacher need not confine his use of reinforcement simply to discussion classes or question and answer sessions. He also uses reinforcement to regulate social behaviour and to give a teaching group or an individual a sense of well-being. Praising a pupil who on one occasion comes early to a class rather than late will encourage him to be a better time keeper. Praising a group after they have tackled a difficult assignment or done some community work will give them a glow of satisfaction. Praising an individual for some achievement in the sports field can give him and his group a feeling of pride. Complimenting an individual on his dress or appearance helps him to feel good. Using their names in a friendly way and showing interest in them as individuals all contribute to promoting a happy friendly class who will be more willing to work. One must, of course, choose the appropriate moments and settings to use positive reinforcement. To tell a girl pupil in front of the whole class that she is looking pretty would embarrass her. To praise an achievement several weeks after it has occurred will be regarded as false or phoney by many pupils. To lavish public approval upon a shy boy's work may actually discourage him from achieving lest he has to go through the embarrassment again. I leave you to decide what would be an appropriate moment or setting in the three examples given in this paragraph.

Some sceptical readers of this unit may find the deliberate use of reinforcement somewhat distasteful. Others may say it is not practical in difficult classes. These criticisms may be answered as follows.

[124]   Successful teachers are usually rated high on warmth, friendliness and enthusiasm. An essential ingredient of these variables is pupil reinforcement. Now that we know this and know that people can be trained in reinforcement techniques it would seem sensible to train teachers in this way so that they can become more successful. The

Activity 34

1. Draw up a list of verbal, non-verbal and extra-verbal reinforcers which teachers could use in microteaching lessons.
2. Listed below are six teaching problems. Write an appropriate verbal statement or question and describe any extra-verbal or non-verbal reinforcements you would use.

    Example: John is a nervous pupil who lacks self confidence. He has just handed in an assignment which is badly written and is not an answer to the question you set.

    Answer: Teacher says quietly (with shake of his head), 'John, I don't think you quite got the point of this assignment. Could we talk it over when I've given the class their next project?'

    1. Last night you read a very perceptive essay on Conrad's *Lord Jim*. Susan, the girl who wrote it, is very bright but inclined to be erratic. Just before the class comes in, she walks into the room.
    b. During a discussion David, who is a shy, withdrawn pupil, raises his hand to make a comment and then lowers it again.
    c. Peter is a below average student in mathematics. The class have been learning how to bisect an angle. You are walking round the class and you see that his work is exceptionally neat and he has almost completed the exercises. Peter looks up and says 'Are these all right, sir?'
    d. During a discussion, Mary asks a very searching question. You remember that Henry, another pupil in the same class, wrote an interesting essay on this topic last week. Give a comment and the non-verbal cues which would reinforce both Mary and Henry.
    e. A pupil is attempting to answer a question. He is doing a good job and he is on the right lines. You want him to know that it's a good answer but you don't want to interrupt him.
    f. For the past ten minutes, a pupil (Stephen) has been dominating a discussion. You want him to stop talking. You don't want him to feel rejected, and you do want someone else to make a contribution.

second criticism is more subtle and telling. It is true that publicly praising an individual in an alienated hostile class may not be effective. The other pupils may laugh and tease the praised pupil. 'Ha, ha, Smithy's a teacher's pet.' Neither Smith nor his classmates might appear to respond to this praise and they may regard the teacher as 'soft'. Nonetheless discreet private praise may gradually win pupils over and praise which sounds grudging may also be effective. 'Mmm. You're not a bad lot. In fact you're doing all right' may sound like faint praise to you. To a rough class it may just be sufficient to begin gradually winning them over. At a later stage it may be necessary to break the class's stereotype image of themselves: 'We're the bad 'uns in this school, sir.' Breaking stereotypes and replacing them with positive self images is not easy. Nonetheless the judicious use of praise will probably be more successful than any other strategy.

Activity 35

1. Read the Pupil Reinforcement Guide Appraisal given on page 126.
2. Plan a microteaching lesson of ten minutes' duration which involves questions, answers and pupil discussion.
3. Teach the lesson using as many different reinforcers, verbal, extra-verbal, and non-verbal, as you can.
4. View the lesson and assess your performance on the guide.
5. Use BIAS to obtain a measure of teacher questions, pupil responses, and teacher responses.
6. Discuss your BIAS analysis with a friend.
7. Write a brief paragraph indicating how you might improve your use of reinforcement.

Pupil participation

The skills of observing pupil behaviour and giving pupil reinforcement contribute to increasing pupil participation. What remains now is to describe 'using pupils' ideas' and 'varying interactions'.

Using pupils' ideas

Using the pupils' own ideas is a special form of reinforcement which appears to be related to pupil achievement and positive attitudes (Rosenshine, 1971; Flanders and Simon, 1969). The ideas may be simply *acknowledged*, they may be *accepted with enthusiasm*, they may be *restated* or towards the end of a discussion they may be *summarized*. The

PUPIL REINFORCEMENT APPRAISAL GUIDE

Please read this guide before you teach and before you view your microlesson. When rating your lesson place a tick in the appropriate box

	Rarely	Sometimes	Almost always
1. You responded to pupil answers and questions with such words as good, fine, splendid			
2. You encouraged pupils to participate by using cues such as ah ha, mmmm, mm'mm, etc.			
3. You encouraged pupils to participate by using such as smiling, nodding your head, writing their answers on the blackboard, looking and listening in a variety of friendly ways			
4. You used prompts and probes to help pupils arrive at appropriate answers			
5. You gave simple directions such as 'Think again', 'Look again', which helped pupils to arrive at appropriate answers			
6. You gave credit for the correct part of a pupil's answer			
7. You linked pupils' responses to other pupil responses made earlier in the lesson			

Skill comments:

pupils' ideas may also be used as a springboard for developing the discussion further. 'That's fine. Now can anyone take Peter's suggestion any further?'

The ideas of different pupils may be compared: 'Ben says . . . and Naomi says . . . What do you think of their ideas, Sheila?'

The above techniques draw pupils into a discussion. When a shy or withdrawn child makes a contribution one should try to use his ideas so that he feels that he can continue to make contributions. When a contribution is partially correct one should try to use the correct part and ignore the remainder.

Varying interactions

Most lessons are one way processes, teacher to pupils. Often so-called discussion lessons are dominated by the teacher. To minimize teacher talk one needs to vary interaction between pupils. This can be done by opening the discussion with a few simple directions. 'Today we are going to discuss the role of the voluntary services. I want you to listen to each other's points and if you want to answer the points you should raise your hand and then explain to the class or the previous speaker why you support or disagree with him.' During the discussion the teacher should avoid too much eye contact with the pupils whilst they are speaking. Naturally, pupils turn to the teacher to see if he approves of what they are saying. Your task is to switch attention from yourself to a pupil. Hence you should look at a pupil who may want to talk. Another tactic is to look backwards and forwards from one pupil to another. This will encourage the pupil speaking to turn towards the other pupil. This in its turn may encourage the listening pupil to speak.

In following these tactics in a large class it is particularly important to direct and distribute questions, looks and request for contributions to all parts of the classroom so that no one section of the class feels isolated or bored. Even the most lively and entertaining discussion must come to an end. Monitor the class particularly after the first five minutes of discussion, summarize the main points made and, if it is appropriate, congratulate the class on the level of discussion. By stopping before the class is bored you capitalize on their enjoyment of discussion – they will want to discuss again. By summarizing the main points they have made you use a powerful form of reinforcement and increase their learning. By congratulating the whole class you reinforce the group image and boost morale.

This unit was designed to develop your skills of gaining pupil participation. If you have read and practised the skills described you will have sharpened your perception of the attending behaviours of pupils, you will have improved your reinforcement skills and you should be able to involve pupils in discussion lessons.

A comment on the teaching skills programme

This course has been concerned with improving your teaching skills. You have tackled activities concerned with planning, perceiving and performing teaching skills, your atten-

Activity 36

1. Plan a microteaching discussion lesson of ten minutes' duration on some controversial aspect of your subject which might appeal to your class. (Example: Why should we learn French?) List some of the questions you may use and indicate some of the points likely to be made in the discussion.
2. Teach the lesson. Use reinforcement and the pupils' ideas, and practise varying the interactions between pupils by means of verbal and non-verbal cues. Summarize the main points of the discussion at the end of the lesson.
3. Do a BIAS analysis of your lesson. Estimate the number of pupil voluntary responses, pupil responses, teacher responses and teacher questions. You could use the BIAS extensions (p. 75).
4. View your lesson with a friend and discuss ways of improving the level of pupil participation.
5. Write a brief paragraph indicating how you might improve your skills of pupil participation.

Activity 37

1. Plan a microteaching lesson of twenty minutes' duration which involves exposition, questioning and discussion skills.
2. Teach the lesson.
3. View the lesson and rate it on the Classroom Guidance Schedule (p. 61).
4. View the lesson again and analyse it using BIAS.
5. Rate your very first lesson with pupils (p. 47) on the Classroom Guidance Schedule. Then analyse it using BIAS.
6. Compare your ratings and analyses of the first and last lessons.
7. Compare also the ratings you gave to the first lesson when you first viewed it and the ratings you give it now.
8. Look over your lesson notes and then write a paragraph indicating any improvements you have made in teaching. Write a further paragraph in which you pinpoint areas of weakness in your planning and performance skills which require further practice.

tion has been drawn to relevant research and you have read suggestions and hints for improving your teaching in classrooms as well as in microteaching laboratories.

The course was intended as a preliminary to class teaching. Before embarking upon teaching in the classroom you should tackle the last activity of the programme. This will help you to determine whether your planning has improved, your perceptions have changed and your performance is more effective.

Section Three

Organising a microteaching programme

This section is largely concerned with ways of setting up a microteaching programme. It describes methods of organizing the equipment and laboratories; how to timetable students and supervising tutors and it puts forward suggestions for the supervision of microteaching. The sections ends with a brief discussion of ways of modifying and extending the basic skills programme.

Costs and equipment

Almost the first question one is asked about microteaching is 'How much does it cost?' No simple answer is possible although some guidelines are given in this section. Prices vary throughout the world; you may choose simple or complex set-ups; you may decide to use videotape for some skills, audiotape for others and no equipment for others; you can make do without separate playback and viewing facilities or you can have fully equipped viewing seminar rooms; you may use peer group teaching only, pupil teaching only, or both, and you may want trainees to microteach once, twice, or more times per week. Finally you have to weigh the costs and payoffs of microteaching against that of alternatives such as school experience.

This last point is worth considering in more detail. As long ago as 1965 Sir Alec Clegg wrote, 'I cannot believe that a visit to a school or group of schools which can cost as much as £20 in the tutor's salary and a further £20 in travelling expenses is not something we could not do as efficiently in other ways.' (Clegg, 1965, 'Dangers Ahead', *Education*, p. 240.) To these costs must be added student travel, meals and accommodation which in 1968 were about £14 per student per year (Helm, 1970). By 1974 the costs of organizing a school practice which includes the salaries of the organizing tutor and secretary is almost certainly over £20 per student per year in Britain. In East Africa the average costs per student per year is about £70, or two and a half times the national average income. In New Guinea, where some students have to be flown out to teaching practice schools, the costs are over £100 per student per year. The capital costs of one fully equipped microteaching laboratory and viewing room which would comfortably throughput sixty student microlessons per week could be recouped well within two years in Great Britain and in far less time in developing countries. The laboratory would contain two fixed cameras, microphones and standard classroom equipment. Its control room would contain one half inch videotape recorder, three monitors and camera switching gear. The viewing seminar room would contain a monitor and a half inch videotape recorder. There would be ample videotape and sufficient money for spare components. (It is wise to include a figure of 10 per cent of the cost for spares if one is indenting for capital expenditure. This will cover costs during the first five years.) The laboratory and viewing rooms may also be used for in-service and curriculum development work and studies of group behaviour, as well as for microteaching.

A class of thirty pupils may be split into five or six microclasses providing there is adequate space and facilities. (You can use larger groups, of course.) In a half day, each microclass can give up to fifteen minutes' experience to eight students. The pupils enjoy the experience particularly if it is a regular weekly event. No precise equivalences of micro-teaching and school experience are available. Gibbs of Callender Park College, Falkirk and McIntyre of the University of Stirling are investigating this issue. In the meantime the work of Kallenbach and Gall (1969) suggests that a skill demonstration to a year group followed by one or two sessions of microteaching and viewing with a supervisor is equivalent to one day's experience in school. This estimate is probably only valid for the initial stages of training.

In contrast, one can usually only allocate one or two students per whole class in a conventional teaching practice – and the students do not have the advantage of seeing themselves teach or the help of a supervisor during their first attempts. The problems of placing students in schools are reduced if microteaching replaces one school practice. The costs of transporting a class of pupils to the college or university is considerably less than the cost of transporting forty or more students to different schools. The pressure upon school staff and supervisors is reduced. The use of a college-based and a school-based practice is not new (see McNair, 1964). Staffs of schools and colleges can be drawn more closely together to develop ways of introducing students to teaching. Attention can be given to the question, 'What skills should a student have acquired before he begins teaching whole classes?' Those who prefer to throw people in at the deep end might argue none. More humane, insightful teachers and tutors can attempt joint action research. The spin-off of mutual learning is in itself worth the effort and there is nothing quite like a videotape of a student's microlesson for sparking off vigorous discussions of teaching.

All of this may seem a far cry from the question, 'How much does it cost?' but social costs and benefits are at least as important as the actual costs of equipment. The following notes are a rough and ready guide based on prices in 1974 in Britain.

MICROPHONES

Multidirectional microphones are better than stick microphones. They are best suspended from the ceiling rather than placed on stands. Avoid placing them on the teacher's and pupils' desks or tables for they pick up extraneous noise. (Price range: £20–25)

CAMERAS

Make sure they are sensitive enough for the lighting of the room. Alternatively increase the illumination of the room. If the camera is to be fixed, make sure it has a wide angle lens. (Price range: £180–200; wide-angle lens £20–25)

SWITCH GEAR/MIXERS

If more than one camera is used, you need to buy switch gear or mixers. The simplest and cheapest cuts from one camera to the other. A competent technician can make this equipment. More sophisticated devices for fading one camera out or mixing pictures taken by two cameras may be bought. They enable you to see teacher and pupil behaviour simultaneously. (Price range: £20–300)

VIDEOTAPE RECORDERS

Sizes vary from $\frac{1}{4}$ in to 2 in. Reel or cassette are available. $\frac{1}{2}$ in reel videotape recorder are the most widely used. It is best to stick to one type – and ensure that all your machines are compatible. $\frac{1}{2}$ in recorders are now available with variable playback speeds so you can watch the non-verbal signals of critical incidents in slow motion. Portable battery/mains packs of videotape recorders are available but they are not as robust as the standard equipment. (Price range: Standard $\frac{1}{2}$ in £400–450; portable $\frac{1}{2}$ in with camera £750)

MONITORS

Sizes vary from $1\frac{1}{2}$ in to 27 in. 9 in monitors are suitable for control rooms but a larger monitor (23 in) is preferable for use in the viewing room. (Price range: £90–120)

ANCILLARY EQUIPMENT

Sets of leads for direct re-recording, dubbing and editing are useful. Make sure you have spare sets of videorecorder heads. Cans of anti-static fluid for cleaning video heads should be purchased – and used regularly. Check that you have sufficient plugs in the rooms to be used for microteaching and adequate storage space for spare tapes and components. If no rooms can be wired permanently for microteaching use, all the equipment may be stored on a trolley – which can easily be made from angle iron and chipboard. Alternatively the camera may be fixed in the room and the trolley used for a monitor and videotape recorder. After microteaching the videorecorder is unplugged from the camera and wheeled on the trolley to another room (preferably on the same floor!) for viewing.

Readers who are thinking of using videotape equipment in tropical conditions should read the note in Appendix B.

Setting up the laboratories

Each microteaching laboratory should be well lit, well ventilated and well equipped with blackboards, display boards, an overhead projector, a sink, ample 3-point plugs and light movable classroom furniture. Carpet or soft rubber flooring cuts down undesirable noise and it is worth the extra expense. Trolleys of basic equipment and materials for science, environmental studies, creative arts etc. are worth devising. Alternatively each microteaching laboratory may be equipped with materials and apparatus suitable for one area of curriculum work.

One high quality microphone suspended from the ceiling between the teacher and pupils is usually sufficient for a microclass of five or six pupils sitting close together – provided that extraneous noises such as air conditioning are minimal. If the room is to be permanently wired it is worth having up to four microphones and a sound mixer in the control room. This enables you to use the laboratory for teaching larger groups and for experimenting with team teaching and organizing group learning.

If only one fixed camera is used, it is best hung high on the wall or on the ceiling in front of the teacher and pupils who should be seated in a horse-shoe shape. This shows both teacher and pupil non-verbal signals. Figure 11 shows the set-up. Figure 12 shows a two camera set-up. Wide angle lenses should be used for both cameras. It is also possible to use remote controlled cameras for tracking teacher or pupil movements but for most training situations this is not necessary. You should as far as possible avoid having camera operators in the microteaching laboratory. They can distract

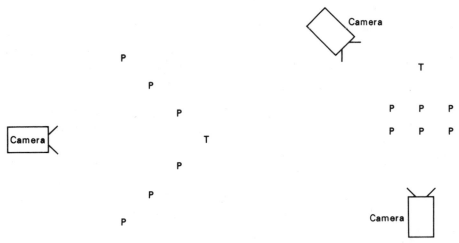

Figure 11. One camera set-up   Figure 12. Two camera set-up

teachers and pupils and they become obsessed with quality television productions whereas the correct focus is improving the quality of the student's teaching behaviour. You may also need to re-emphasize this point with some CCTV technicians.

All microteaching laboratories should be fitted with a time signalling device which can be operated from the control room. A flashing light or a soft toned buzzer are best. Loud bells are disturbing to people working in other laboratories.

The microteaching laboratories may be monitored from one control room or each laboratory could have its own well insulated control room. The latter is preferable since each laboratory may be used independently, the control room can be used to watch live teaching and students can learn to handle the relatively simple switchgear necessary for one set-up. Each control room should have a stop clock for timing lessons. The viewing rooms should be insulated from the laboratories to avoid double recording. They should contain comfortable seats so that viewing and discussion may be relaxed and they should preferably be large enough for seminars on modelling and protocol materials (taped or written examples of teaching) as well as for microteaching critique sessions. The weekly timetables for the use of the viewing rooms should be posted on the doors so that users know when they are free for private study.

One room should be set aside for the videotape library and microteaching co-ordinators' room. The co-ordinator or co-ordinators may be graduate students. If there is a heavy commitment to microteaching, it is worth appointing a part-time technical assistant responsible for co-ordinating supervisor, student and pupil time-tables, making sure that materials and rating schedules are available and keeping records of the videotape library.

Each tape should be numbered and a register of tapes kept which shows the following information

Tape No:
Student:
Seen by supervisor:
Date of recording:
Skill:
Date erased:

On loan (to whom, when and date returned):

The names of the student and the rev. counts for the beginning of each of their lessons should also be recorded on the videotape boxes on sticky labels which are easily peeled off.

If a large number of pupils are involved in microteaching it is worth setting aside a reception room containing books and other learning materials so that the children may be profitably occupied during any spare time they may have. Sometimes it is possible for the pupils to continue working independently on the theme introduced by the students in the microlessons.

Figure 13. Plan of N.U.U. microteaching laboratories (not to scale)

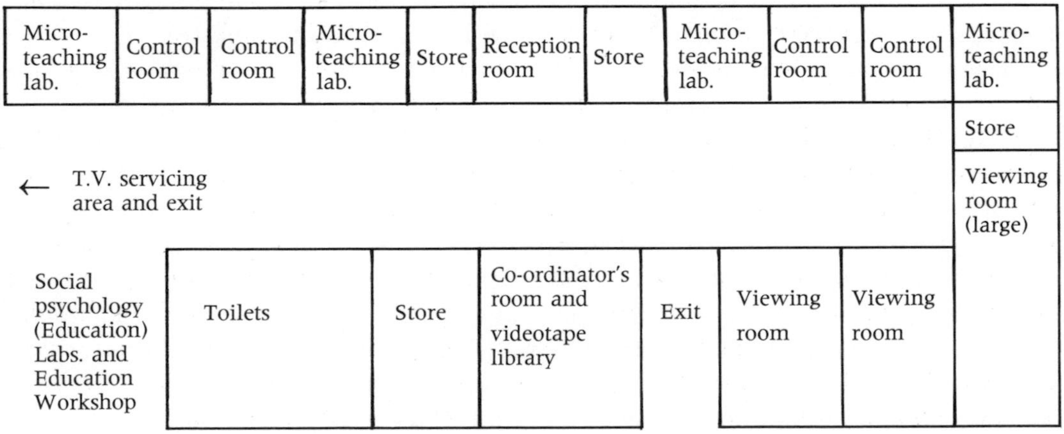

Micro-teaching lab.	Control room	Control room	Micro-teaching lab.	Store	Reception room	Store	Micro-teaching lab.	Control room	Control room	Micro-teaching lab.
										Store
← T.V. servicing area and exit										Viewing room (large)
Social psychology (Education) Labs. and Education Workshop	Toilets		Store	Co-ordinator's room and videotape library		Exit	Viewing room	Viewing room		

Figure 13 shows the plan of the New University of Ulster's microteaching laboratories. [137] You will note that store rooms occur between each microteaching laboratory and control room.

Timetabling the practical programme

This section describes a way of timetabling supervisors, students and pupils based upon the module of student team teaching used in this programme (see also Young, 1970). Reteach sessions *immediately after* teaching and viewing do not seem to warrant the extra cost and administrative difficulties. And students do not appear to enjoy or benefit from immediate reteach sessions (Berliner, 1969; Brown, 1973; Brown and Gibbs, 1974).

If this is the first venture of the college into microteaching it is advisable to hold informal meetings with tutors, principals (head teachers) and school staff to introduce them to the ideas, if possible, to show them some examples of videotaped lessons and to give them the opportunity of making suggestions about the possible programme. Principals often are understandably concerned about the benefit their pupils will derive from the experience and supervisors about the benefits for students. The key to success in these discussions lies in carefully thought-out compromises. It is worth gently pointing out at such meetings that one has to balance the needs of various curriculum areas, pressures upon staff and organizational problems *vis-à-vis* schools and the whole course. Compromise on some issues is essential if one is to develop an efficient and effective programme.

Six questions need to be answered before starting on the timetable. First, how long will each microlesson be? Second, how many times per week will the students teach? Third, will supervisors be viewing and discussing all their students' lessons? Fourth, will students be working in teams drawn from the same curriculum areas? Fifth, will pupils be involved in the whole of the microteaching programme? Sixth, how many pupils will be involved? The answers to these questions will be partly determined by the college or university timetable and the availability of pupils.

If this is a first venture, I suggest that one should try to gain agreement on microlessons of 10–15 minutes. This uses one reel of tape per team of four students. Students should teach one lesson per week and supervisors should be involved in viewing and discussing all lessons; that, as far as possible, the teams are drawn from the same curriculum area and that school pupils are involved after the completion of Unit II. This simplifies organization, fits most college timetables and probably satisfies the most pressing demands of staff and students.

The students are usually more difficult to timetable than supervisors or pupils. It is therefore suggested that this problem should be tackled first. If only small numbers are involved the task is easy. They should be asked to sign up in teams of four within their own curriculum area for the times and laboratories available. On a typical schoolday one might use the times 9.00–10.30; 10.30–12.00; 1.15–2.30; 2.30–3.45. This allows time for supervising children during breaks and the journeys to and from schools. The lectures/social skills demonstrations should be held at a time when there is no microteaching practice.

When many students are involved they can be asked to:

   (i) Consult with their peers within the same curriculum area and form themselves into teams of four.

 (ii) Each complete a blank microteaching timetable indicating when they are free. Write their own names on the timetable and underline them. Write the names of the rest of the team.

(iii) Hand in the set of timetables for each team – so that the microteaching co-ordinator does not have to sort the timetables into teams.

The co-ordinator should then read the timetables and note the most popular hours and days. He should then choose the time and day for each team's practice session and pencil it in on a master timetable. He should avoid using the popular hours and days until he is well through the task. When no common time is available for a team, the team should be split. The provisional timetable produced will probably require modification at least once. When the provisional timetable is completed, a *copy* of it should be placed on a notice board with a note advising students that they should contact you immediately on that day if a timetable change is necessary.

The next step is to allocate students to supervisors. If small numbers of students are involved, the provisional timetable can be shown to supervisors so that they can choose their team. They can then make arrangements with the team for mutually convenient viewing and discussion times (one hour per team) and write these times on the timetables for the viewing rooms. It is not necessary for supervisors to be present during the actual teaching although many supervisors prefer to do this and then to immediately view and discuss the lessons.

If several staff are involved and timetabling is extremely difficult they should be personally contacted and a timetable completed for each member of staff indicating when he is available for supervision and his time preferences. A master timetable of viewing times for each team and for supervisors should then be prepared. The two timetables should then be matched. This procedure is cumbersome and computerization does not appear to save labour on this problem. The procedure should only be used as a last resort. If timetabling is so complex that supervisors and teams of students cannot meet for one hour per week to discuss teaching then it is worth examining the overall commitments of staff and students in the college or department to other courses. It may even be worth reappraising the structure of the whole course.

The next step is to finalize arrangements for pupils to come to the college. If you have the space and facilities it is better to involve whole classes for half-days. This gives a large throughput of students and minimizes disruption of the school timetable. School principals are usually very helpful and co-operative if they have been consulted well beforehand. Primary school classes can be accompanied by their class teacher. The advice and encouragement they give to students is often valuable. The teachers frequently enjoy the experience of watching students work with small groups of their children and very often discover new facets of the children's personalities.

When the arrangements are completed the final timetable including the names of supervisors and the school classes should be published.

During the microteaching programme, make sure that staff, technical staff and students are informed if children are not available for microteaching – because of, for example, half-term holidays. At the end of the programme a letter of thanks should be sent to the principals and staff of the co-operating schools and a meeting arranged to discuss the microteaching programme. The letter is particularly important if teacher tutors are involved in the next phase of the students' training – experience in schools.

Training in the use of equipment

All students and supervisors should be taught how to:

    (i) Switch on the equipment
   (ii) thread a tape recorder (or load a cassette);
  (iii) record and playback a lesson;
  (iv) set the rev. counter on the VTR;
   (v) adjust the controls on the monitor.

The equipment should be checked to ensure it is recording before it is used for the microteaching recording. At the beginning of the first lesson on the tape the revolution (rev.) counter should be set to zero. The lessons should be timed and the appropriate revs written on the label. At the end of the team's session the tape should be rewound, placed in its box and returned to the microteaching co-ordinator.

It is worth emphasizing to participants that they should consult a technician if there is any fault in the equipment. Amateur attempts at servicing can prove expensive and disruptive. The students should be reminded to rotate the order in which they teach and handle the equipment.

The role of the supervisor in microteaching

Put simply, the role of the supervisor is to help a student to improve his own teaching. His role therefore subtly changes during the training programme. In the early stages he usually needs to be particularly encouraging and supportive. As the student learns to analyse and improve his skills the supervisor gradually withdraws his support – but not his encouragement. By the end of the programme the student should be able to analyse and suggest improvements with virtually no help from the supervisor. In short, the supervisor should try to work himself out of a job.

Let it be said at once that this approach is not based upon research evidence. Research evidence on the role of the supervisor is, at best, equivocal. (McAleese and Unwin, 1971; Griffiths, 1972). So much so that Borg and his associates (1970) argue that supervisors may be unnecessary. This is probably true of inservice teachers but not of teachers in training. Johnson and Knaupp (1970) found that students expected their supervisors to be qualified to render assistance and that they, the students, should have an opportunity for self-guided professional development. The factor analysis of students' responses to the Likert-type attitude scale also indicated that they liked to share the experiences with peers and to have their strengths appreciated and faults overlooked. Similar views were expressed by students at Ulster. A sample of some of their comments are printed on page 142. They are worth considering by anyone concerned with supervisor-student relationships.

The students at Ulster and at Stirling were also firmly convinced of the need for supervision (Brown and Gibbs, 1974; McIntyre and Duthie, 1971). Their expectations and wishes may not be typical of all students. Nor are students' expectations and wishes in themselves a sufficient basis for an effective programme – but a programme which does not take them into account is less likely to succeed. For these reasons we applied at Ulster the Listen (question and summarize) and Tell technique recommended by Maier (1958) in his text on appraisal interviews.

Maier lists three general strategies: Tell, Listen and Tell, and Listen (non-directive counselling). Telling often leads to superficial compliance, and Listening leads rapidly to changes in behaviour but not necessarily in the direction desired by the listener. This leaves Listen and Tell. This allows students to develop their own analytical skills and to suggest their own approaches. At the same time the supervisor can prompt and suggest to his students ways of improving their skills. Unit III contains an extract from a supervisory session (p. 56). based on the Listen and Tell techniques, and page 141 in this section gives an important *aide-mémoire* for supervisors. If this is a first venture into microteaching then a meeting to discuss methods of supervision is necessary. This is a sensitive area and it requires delicate handling. You are unlikely to gain co-operation by simply telling the supervisors what they must do. Their responses may be of the two word variety or, even worse, superficial compliance. Course co-ordinators should treat the exercise as an important application of the Listen (question and summarize) and Tell technique.

Before leaving this topic, it may be as well to point to an apparent contradiction between the behavioural approaches of microteaching and the counselling approach recommended for the supervisor operating the system. The contradiction is superficial. Both are based upon the principle that positive reinforcement and feedback improve learning. The use of a student's ideas by a supervisor is itself rewarding and encourages a student to supply further analyses and suggestions. Thus by listening, gently probing, summarizing and telling, the supervisor uses a powerful reinforcement technique to direct the student's attention to his central task: improving his own teaching. At the same time, the student is likely to make detailed suggestions which he thinks he can carry out whereas the same detailed suggestions by a supervisor may be overwhelming and appear to the student to be beyond his capabilities.

AN AIDE-MEMOIRE FOR SUPERVISORS

Microteaching supervision

Microteaching begins on .... As indicated in the course outline students will be working in teams of ..... Each team has approximately .... teaching time.

Supervisors are asked to meet their team(s) for ..... hour(s) each week to discuss the skills under review that week and to suggest approaches and topics for the following week's skills. Please use the guides and rating schedules provided in the viewing rooms and hand these, together with the videotape, to the co-ordinator at the end of the viewing session.

When commenting on a student's skill performance you are particularly asked to keep to the guidelines we agreed upon:

1. Read the guides and/or assignments before viewing the microlessons

2. Do not view the whole of the lesson (unless it is the first or last lesson of the programme or one requiring special attention). Instead, sample the beginning, middle and end of the lesson and use the time gained in discussion.

3. As for the students' comments immediately after viewing the lesson. 'What did you think of that?'

4. Ask the group of students how they think the skill may be improved upon

5. Select only one or two main points for discussion which are related to the skills under review. Avoid detailed discussion of other aspects of the lesson unless they are absolutely crucial

6. In discussion, focus upon getting the team to suggest ways of improving performance

7. Summarize the team's views including your own

Remember: A main objective of our programme is to make microteaching a rewarding experience, not an exercise in fault finding. Let me know if any problems arise.

```
                            .........................
                            Microteaching co-ordinator
```

Some comments on supervisors and supervision*

ON SUPERVISORS

1. *Newly appointed supervisors need to be well versed in social skills, have a conviction that their job is worthwhile and be up to date in their knowledge of microteaching and modern methods of teaching.*
2. *Provided that a supervisor knows exactly what he is doing and has a good relationship with his trainees he can be of great assistance, sharpen the perception of the trainee and produce a positive change in teaching behaviour.*
3. *Misconceptions of what the supervisor wants in the trainee has resulted in considerable wasted time and frustration. Stewig (1970) suggests more sensitive approaches are needed before these can be eliminated.*
4. *Supervisors who are experienced teachers tend to impose their ideas on the trainee on how the skill should be exhibited. However the supervisor must also learn to value and focus upon the way the skill is demonstrated by the student.*
5. *If he (the supervisor) doesn't know the objective of the session then he is of little use to the student.*
6. *One final point for supervisors is, just as they expect the students to create an atmosphere for pupil participation they too should develop relationships with their students to show that they practise what they preach.*

ON SUPERVISION

1. *Supervision is greatly helped if objectives are stated in behavioural terms and the supervisors are able to suggest ways of achieving these objectives.*
2. *The function of the supervisor is to make the student into a better teacher. It should not be the function of the student to 'psyche' out what the supervisor's beliefs and intentions are in this matter.*
3. *The third group of learning theories are to do with reward. Learning is held to be superior when it is controlled by reward and it is believed that experiences of success makes criticism easier to accept when it comes. Thus the supervisor in the early stages of training should make the most of the trainee's assets and least of his liabilities.*

Modifying and extending the basic skills programme

A programme of teaching skills for undergraduate and post-graduate certificate students should not rely solely upon this text. At the very least it should contain supplementary lectures and skill demonstrations in which the students play the roles of pupils and afterwards discuss the experience. The skill performance need not always exemplify good teaching. Indeed, there are advantages in occasionally demonstrating an approach which would antagonize pupils or create control problems. Role play and skill demonstration help the students to understand the feelings of pupils, how to carry out the skills and they demonstrate that the lecturer can do what he is asking the students to do. They may be supplemented by videotapes of skill demonstrations and lessons in various curriculum areas. The students' attention should be directed to the salient features of the demonstration and it should be discussed.

* (Taken from some students' answers to a question on microteaching supervisors and supervision. New University of Ulster, 1972.)

Such demonstrations and discussions also give students ideas to use in microteaching.
In fact one of their most pressing problems is what to teach. After the first few lessons they rapidly run out of ideas. To avoid this, one can get the teams of students to brainstorm series of topics at the beginning of the programme. Alternatively, lesson packs which are suitable for exposition, discussion and discovery lessons in various curriculum areas can be devised. This is a time consuming task and during the first year of a new programme it may only be possible to produce sample lessons.

Some supervisors and students claim they cannot concentrate solely on one skill per lesson. If this is the case, you might split the practical programme into clusters of skills (for example, four sessions on each of exposition, questioning, discussion methods) and devise suitable assignments and rating schedules based on skill clusters. The lecture/skill demonstration can still be directed towards component skills within each cluster and supervisors can be asked to spend some of the time discussing the particular skill under review. The approach appeals to some supervisors but it carries the risk of becoming an exercise in rhetoric by the supervisor and no longer an exercise in professional self-development by the student.

Regardless of whether lesson packs or clusters of skills are used there comes a time when students must independently choose their topics and methods and move into a situation more akin to classroom teaching. If resources are available, the students could be asked to teach longer lessons to larger classes (about half a school class for 30 minutes). The children may be of a different age range from those used in microteaching. The students can be asked to plan a series of lessons on one theme. Samples from the beginning, middle and end of the lesson may be videorecorded for use in supervisory sessions. The supervisor need not view all the videorecordings – that could be left partly to the discretion of the student. Lectures and skill demonstrations should be devoted to the problems of organization, management and control. In addition there should be seminars in which teaching problems are presented and discussed. Some of these may be introduced by the tutor and others may arise directly out of the students' recent teaching. Tutors working in the same fields could devise sets of teaching problems. Bishop and Whitfield (1972) and Perry and Perry (1969) contain some useful suggestions.

This approach introduces students to managerial problems, gives them a safe opportunity to experiment with organizing small groups learning within a larger class and extends their lesson planning and performance skills so that they are even better equipped for organizing and teaching whole classes in schools.

At the next stage teacher tutors, who should have some experience of microteaching, could take over the day to day responsibility for training in schools. It may be worth establishing a joint committee of tutors and teacher-tutors to oversee the microteaching and school experience programme. Supervising tutors could be responsible for the organization and content of the college-based practice, and teacher-tutors for the school based programme. The supervisors could be consultants for the school experience programme and the teacher-tutors the consultants for the teaching skills programme in college. This might help to bring teachers and tutors more closely together in the common enterprise of training teachers.

Microteaching and small group teaching with videotape could be used as a refresher course just before school experience begins or to sharpen up skills during the school experience. Similarly during the first year of teaching, occasional refresher courses with videotape do prove helpful. But more important than the skill training is the opportunity for first year teachers to meet and discuss their teaching problems with helpful, sympathetic teachers and tutors. The first year of teaching is perhaps the most neglected area of training (Collins, 1969; Taylor, 1971; Georgiades, 1972). Very often young teachers are given difficult classes and receive little support from the school or educational authorities. Without such support they learn as best they can the strategies of survival. They may be rapidly socialized into a teaching style and role which many tutors and teachers are not anxious to propagate. All the valuable training experience a student receives may be reduced to nought unless more attention is given to the problems and pitfalls which face young teachers.

A final comment on the programme

Throughout this book the emphasis has been upon the basic skills of teaching. Planning, perception and the performance have been its dominant themes. The approach was based upon the social skills model of teaching described in Section One. In Section Two the approach was outlined in detail. The programme is systematic and explicit. It does produce changes in teaching behaviour. It is thought to be helpful and useful by the students who have used it. It is a move towards integrating psychological, philosophical issues and practical problems in teaching into a common perspective.

The training of teachers is too important a task to be treated haphazardly (see Smith, 1969b.) or hidden in a sandwich of main subjects and theoretical studies in education. By making the programme explicit it is hoped that others may be moved to analyse and construct better and more comprehensive programmes. For many problems await solution (for example, the role of the supervisor, when to use video or audio feedback). Producing changes in teaching behaviour is not enough. Teaching skills are only worthwhile insofar as they produce desirable changes in pupil learning and attitudes. The term 'desirable' like many terms in the study of teaching is inescapably value-laden. The paths to desirable pupil learning are many. The need for a perspective to help students and teachers to evaluate these issues is pressing. The value of such a perspective rests ultimately on its capacity to sustain teachers in their moments of crisis, to help them to refine and clarify their experience and to solve their teaching problems. Teaching skills programmes such as the one described in these pages are but a first tentative step. In taking the next step we should continue to bear in mind the moral of the tale told in the preface to this book − 'it is great folly to put one to school to learn any subtle science which hath no natural wit'. The clever Oxford scholar seemed unaware of this maxim and lost his supper. Our losses may be infinitely greater.

Suggested answers and comments

Page 25 (Activity 3)
E.O. = educational objectives; E.I. = explicit instructional objectives; I.I. = implicit instructional objectives.
   The italicized phrase *best described as* is important.

a. E.I.
b. I.I.
c. E.I. – a genuine one.
d. I.I.
e. E.O.
f. E.O.
g. A rogue case. I would place it as a truncated E.I.
h. E.I. – but at what level of cricket playing?
i. E.O.
j. E.O.
k. E.O.

Page 26
c. is the only accurate E.I.

Page 27 (Activity 4)
√ = present   × = absent

a. √ × × √ ×
b. × × × × ×
c. √ √ √ √ √
d. √ √ √ √ √
e. √ √ √ √ √
f. × × √ × ×
g. × × √ × ×
h. √ √ √ √ √
i. √ √ √ √ √
j. × × × × ×
k. √ √ × √ √
l. √ √ × √ √
m. × × √ × ×
n. √ √ √ √ √
o. √ √ √ √ √

Page 28 (Activity 5)
Writing explicit objectives makes you think of the level of performance expected of the pupils. This in its turn forces you to think about what the pupils are likely to know. Only one example for each item is given. There are many more.
   By the end of the teaching episode the pupils will be able to:

1. Read a children's news sheet in French with the aid of a dictionary.
2. Solve simple equations of the type $3x + 5 = 14$ and $5x - 7 = 23$ (without reference to a text book?).
3. Describe the main plot of Hamlet in their own words. Do a pen portrait of the main characters in the play giving recalled quotations to support their views.
4. Organize and conduct a debate with minimal support from the teacher.
5. Identify the essential features of prose and poetry.
6. Play an elementary game of chess. Decide whether nine demonstrated moves in chess are allowable. (It is arguable whether one must play a game to understand it and whether playing is sufficient for understanding. The answer rests upon your implicit notion of understanding.)
7. Distinguish five paintings of Van Gogh from five by a group of his contemporaries. Describe in words and line diagrams the main features of Van Gogh's style.
8. Describe in diagrams and words the physical layout of the neighbourhood. Describe in words, diagrams and models the main physical and social features of the neighbourhood.

    9. Solve three simple problems based upon the laws of reflection. State the laws of reflection and apply them to a given problem.

10. Prepare a small quantity of hydrochloric acid from the range of chemicals and apparatus presented. Describe in words and diagrams a simple experiment (apparatus, quantities of chemicals, methods and precautions) to prepare hydrochloric acid.

11. Identify the probable main effects of the Civil War upon the legal constitution of the United States. List the immediate (probable) effects of the American Civil War upon the United States economy.

12. List and comment upon the main effects on children aged four and under of different types of maternal care including absence of a mother figure.

Page 45 (Activity 9)
1. c; 2. b; 3. a; 4. b; 5. c.

Page 45
Why was such a simple definition of a concept chosen? – So that you would grasp the essential features of a concept.

Page 52 (Activity 12a)
Example 1   *Low inference*: 'Teacher looks', 'A boy calls out'.
                    High inference: 'not very friendly', 'class looks stunned', 'appears to consider it'.
Example 2   *Low inference*: 'Teacher wrote some of them down', 'Almost all hands go up', 'erases the question about belting'.
                    High inference: 'Teacher likes this suggestion', 'The children are a bit excited', 'lots of enthusiastic agreement'.

Page 68 (Activity 16)
Section 1
1. X   Reprimand.
2. TR   Accepts pupils' excitement.
3. TQ   Can be paraphrased as a question. The teacher's intention may be to find out if Susan knows. If you are very certain that it is simply to revise what has gone before it could be coded as TL – giving directions.
4. TR
5. TR
6. TR
7. X   Reprimand.
8. X   Reprimand.
9. PV unless teacher has said, 'Put up your hand when you've finished.'
10. PV
11. PV
12. PV
13. PR if it is in answer to a question.
14. PV   The answer to the question is: A lot. By analysing teaching in this way you learn which moves to make – just as football and tennis players improve their game by analysis as well as practice.

Section 2
1. TL   It may look like builds on pupil ideas, but it is recapitulation.   2. TQ
3. S   4. TQ   5. S   6. PV   7. S   8. TR   9. X (self reproof)
10. X (self reproof)   11. TQ   12. PR   13. TR   14. TQ

Page 70 (Activity 17)
Section 1
Suggest you map out the answers on a time-line display.
1. X (first category is always X)   2. X (Good morning . . .)   3. TL   4. TL
5. TL   6. TL   7. TL   8. TL   9. TL   10. TL   11. TL   12. TL
13. TL   14. TL   15. TL   16. TL   17. TL   18. TL   19. PV   20. TR
21. PV   22. PV   23. PV (note teacher did not intend this question from the student)
24. X (if you code as TR then you must include laughter in the category description)
25. TR   26. TR   27. TR   28. TQ   29. PR

Section 2
This is about as close as we can get to the classroom situation without resort to tape.
Again map out the extract on a time-line display.
1. X (first code)   2. TL   3. TL   4. TQ   5. PR   6. TQ   7. PR
8. TQ   9. TQ   10. S   11. X (it is not a pupil verbal response)
12. TQ (student expects an answer)   13. PR   14. TQ   15. PV   16. TQ
17. PV   18. PV (student did not intend this comment from the pupils)   19. TR
20. PR   21. TR   22. TR   23. X   24. TQ   25. PR
26. TQ (student expects an answer)   27. PR   28. PV   29. TR   30. PR
31. TQ   32. X (pupil response)   33. TQ   34. PR   35. TR   36. TR

Page 74 (Activity 19)
BIAS clues of unplanned lessons: unpredictable silences (S) in the middle of teacher talk; several
TQ followed by TL; very lengthy string of TL; a line of TQ or a zigzag of TQ and silence with
no intervening PR; several PV or PR followed by S's. Very high speed or slow speed teacher
delivery is an extra clue.

Page 86
If the class gets noisy: Pause and stare, talk quietly, switch activities.
    To prevent excessive noise: Excessive noise is often a symptom of poor planning in microteach-
ing. (It *may* be a symptom of organizational problems in a school.) Plan interesting activities,
use systematic, controlled teaching behaviour during class. Direct and distribute questions.
Pupils usually need a clearly defined routine. Explicit training of the pupils in classroom
organization is often required.

Page 94
To arouse pupils' interest in a book. Hold it up, point to sections of particular interest. Talk
animatedly about it. Lean forward slightly with eyes open wide. (Yes!) In short, be enthusiastic.

Page 106
Shy child's completely wrong answer. Without frowning say very quietly, 'No, not quite right',
give the answer and add, 'Isn't it?' When pupil nods say, 'That's right.' Later on in lesson
look to see if he is ready to answer. If he is, try again, and if he is correct praise him (again
quietly and discreetly).

Page 110
Question on Europe's future: synthesis.

Page 112 (Activity 29)
First two questions were not cognitive, so classified as U. Full list is: a. U; b. U; c. R; d. R;

e. R; f. C; g. C (if considering repeats as new questions in the same category, otherwise U); h. R; i. C; j. C. The C categorizations are based on the assumption that most of these points have been covered in recent lessons. If they had not, the C would be categorized as analysis questions. Number of cognitive questions: 8.

Page 114 (Activity 30)
Some possible answers are:

1. Why is Amsterdam the largest city in Holland? (Analysis)
2. Which aspects of *Catcher in the Rye* suggest that the author is a young man? (Analysis)
3. Why is the theorem of Pythagorus so important in geometry? (Evaluation)
4. Describe the feelings of Hamlet for his mother as portrayed in the play by Shakespeare. (Synthesis)
5. What kind of relationship did Scrooge have with his employee in *A Christmas Carol*? (Analysis)
6. Why is oxygen the most common element found in the earth's crust? (Analysis)
7. Account for the distribution of two of the most widely spoken languages in Africa. (Analysis)
8. Discuss the recent theories of the stone formation at Stonehenge. (Evaluation)
9. Why has there been a sudden increase in the number of independent countries in Africa during the past twenty years? (Evaluation)
10. Which type of question do you consider the most important? (Evaluation)

Note that questions need not be written in the interrogative form.

Page 118
Why should a teacher use some higher order questions? – Obviously to encourage pupils (of any age) to think about values, concepts and evidence.

Appendices

Appendix A: Lesson Appraisal Guide

Description

Please read this guide description before observing the student teacher and pupils during the lesson.

Skill in gaining pupils attention

7 indicates that student very effectively gained the pupils' attention before he began teaching.
1 indicates he failed to do so.

Skill in explaining and narrating

7 indicates he explained ideas very lucidly and/or narrated imaginatively.
1 indicates his explanation was totally confused and/or his narration was very dull.

Skill in giving directions

7 indicates his directions were readily understood by the pupils.
1 indicates his directions were totally confusing to the pupils.

Skill in asking and adapting questions to pupils

7 indicates student asked questions which were relevant and interesting and quickly adapted them if pupils did not understand.
1 indicates student asked irrelevant questions and failed to adapt them, if pupils did not understand.

Skill in recognizing pupils' difficulties of understanding

7 indicates student quickly noted when the class or individual pupils had not understood.
1 indicates a total unawareness of pupils difficulties of understanding.

Quality of voice and speech habits

7 indicates student's voice was well modulated and he had few annoying speech habits such as Um, er, Well, etc.
1 indicates student's voice was a monotone and barely audible and he had several annoying speech habits.

Use of non-verbal cues

7 indicates the student used facial expressions, hand movements, eye contact to convey meaning effectively.
1 indicates the student was totally wooden and expressionless.

Skill in encouraging appropriate responses

7 indicates student encouraged pupil answers by phrases such as That's good, Yes, you're right or by non-verbal cues.
1 indicates total absence of encouragement.

Skill in holding pupils' attention

7 indicates student was quick to notice when pupils were bored and changed the activity.
1 indicates student did not notice when pupils were bored.

Skill in gaining pupil participation

7 indicates student got the pupils actively involved in the content of the lesson.
1 indicates student failed to involve the pupils in the content of the lesson.

Skill in controlling the pupils

7 indicates that the student successfully controlled the class of pupils by his remarks, interesting approach or his use of non-verbal cues.

1 indicates that the student totally failed to control the class.

Use of aids. (Blackboard, projections, illustrative materials etc.)

7 indicates that student used his aids sensibly and skilfully.

1 indicates that student used no aids or used them ineffectively.

Allocation of time for pupil learning

7 indicates that student gave the pupils opportunities to ask questions, discuss or do some individual work.

1. indicates that student lectured for the whole lesson.

Lesson planning and structure

7 indicates that the student's actual teaching (*not his notebook*) was well planned and systematic.

1 indicates that the student was disorganized and no plan was detectable.

STUDENT LESSON APPRAISAL GUIDE

Student: Class:

School: Topic:

Date:
(State whether 1st, 2nd or   Observer/Teacher:
 3rd observation)

Observe the student-teacher and pupils carefully during the lesson
and then complete the Student Lesson Appraisal Guide. Assess the
student on each separate item as if he was about to qualify as a
teacher. In cases of doubt always give the extreme ratings (1 and 2;
6 and 7) rather than those in the middle of the scale. Put a ring
round the number which most closely indicates your view of the
student-teacher's performance. 1 is a low score and 7 a high score.

1.   Skill in gaining the pupils' attention | 1 | 2 | 3 | 4 | 5 | 6 | 7 |

2.   Skill in explaining and narrating | 1 | 2 | 3 | 4 | 5 | 6 | 7 |

3.   Skill in giving directions | 1 | 2 | 3 | 4 | 5 | 6 | 7 |

4.   Skill in asking and adapting questions to | 1 | 2 | 3 | 4 | 5 | 6 | 7 |
     pupils

5.   Skill in recognizing pupils' difficulties | 1 | 2 | 3 | 4 | 5 | 6 | 7 |
     of understanding

6.   Quality of voice and speech habits | 1 | 2 | 3 | 4 | 5 | 6 | 7 |

7.   Use of non-verbal cues (e.g. gestures and | 1 | 2 | 3 | 4 | 5 | 6 | 7 |
     facial expressions)

8.   Skill in encouraging appropriate pupil | 1 | 2 | 3 | 4 | 5 | 6 | 7 |
     responses

9.   Skill in holding pupils' attention | 1 | 2 | 3 | 4 | 5 | 6 | 7 |

10. Skill in gaining the participation of | 1 | 2 | 3 | 4 | 5 | 6 | 7 |
     the pupils

11.   Skill in controlling the pupils

1	2	3	4	5	6	7

12.   Use of aids (Blackboards, projectors, illustrative materials etc.)

1	2	3	4	5	6	7

13.   Allocation of time for pupil learning

1	2	3	4	5	6	7

14.   Lesson planning and structure - as <u>performe</u>d by the student-teacher

1	2	3	4	5	6	7

SCORE (please leave blank)

<u>Comments</u>:

Appendix B: Using VTR equipment in the tropics

Heat, humidity and insects can damage equipment, even if it has been tropicalized. As far as possible all VTR equipment should be kept in air conditioned rooms. Taking equipment in and out of air conditioning rapidly ruins it. Hot humid atmospheres make the equipment warm and damp. The air conditioning produces condensation which short-circuits the equipment and perishes any parts made of rubber.

If no air conditioning is available, the equipment should be stored in desiccators (sealed containers) or well ventilated insect-proof cupboards. Check the desiccators regularly to ensure the desiccating agent is not exhausted. Remove all leather and plastic cases before placing the equipment in the desiccators or cupboard. Leather is a breeding ground for fungi. Insects are attracted to plastics (including the plastic on wires). Wax leather or plastic covers and then lightly dust with an insecticide.

The cupboards should contain open shelves. A small heater or electric lamp should be placed in the bottom of the cupboard to circulate the air. Rice in an open mesh bag is a useful drying agent. The bags of rice should be sprayed with insecticide and placed alongside the equipment. The upper part of the cupboards should be used for sensitive equipment.

Videotape recorders, cameras and monitors are sensitive, finely adjusted instruments. They should never be left uncovered when not in use. Lenses are particularly prone to fungi. Parts which require oiling should be oiled *lightly*. Oil evaporates and then condenses in inappropriate parts of the equipment. Use transistor operated equipment rather than valves wherever possible. Transistors usually generate less heat so ventilation whilst the equipment is being used is not as serious a problem. It is nonetheless advisable to use electric fans near all VTRs. This may mean having the VTR some distance from the microphones so that the noise of the fan is not recorded. If you use battery operated equipment then you must check the casings of the batteries regularly to avoid damage due to corrosion. Sealed batteries which require recharging are preferable to disposable ones.

The equipment should be checked daily and the magnetic heads of the VTR lightly sprayed with antistatic fluid after every twelve hours of use. These simple precautions will help you to keep equipment in good working order. You should also consult with the other institutions which are using equipment in similar conditions. They may be able to supply you with lists of components which are important to have readily available. One final word of advice – appoint a competent technician to look after the laboratories and equipment – and take notice of what he says about equipment and laboratory organization.

Bibliography

ABERCROMBIE, M. L. J. (1971) *Aims and Techniques of Group Teaching*, Society for Research in Higher Education.

ADAMS, R. S. and BIDDLE, B. J. (1970) *Realities of Teaching: Explorations with Videotape*, Holt, Rinehart & Winston.

ALLEN, D. W. and FORTUNE, J. C. (1966) 'An analysis in microteaching: New procedure in teacher education', *Microteaching: A Description*, School of Education, Stanford University.

ALLEN, D. W. and RYAN, K. A. (1969) *Microteaching*, Addison-Wesley.

AMIDON, E. J. and HOUGH, J. B., eds. (1967) *Interaction Analysis: Theory Research and Applications*, Addison-Wesley.

ANDREWS, R. (1971) 'Microteaching methods: a critique', *University of London Institute of Education Bulletin*, **23**, 21–30.

ANNETT, J. (1969) *Feedback and Human Performance*, Penguin.

ARGYLE, M. (1970) *Social Interaction*, Methuen.

ARGYLE, M. and KENDON, A. (1967) 'The experimental analysis of social performance', in BERKOWITZ, L, ed. *Advances in Experimental Social Psychology*, Vol. 3.

ASSOCIATION FOR STUDENT TEACHING (1964) *The College Supervisor: Conflict and Challenge*, 43rd Yearbook.

ASPY, D. N. (1972) 'An Investigation into the relationship between teacher's factual knowledge of learning theory and their classroom performance', *J. Tchr. Educ.*, **23**, 21–4.

AUBERTINE, H. (1964) 'An experiment in the set induction process and its application in teaching', Doctoral thesis, Stanford, California.

AUSTAD, C. A. (1972) 'Personality correlates of teacher performance in a microteaching laboratory', *J. Exper. Educ.*, **40**, 1–5.

AUSUBEL, D. P. (1968) *Educational Psychology, A Cognitive View*, Holt, Rinehart & Winston.

BAKER, J. R. (1967) 'A teacher co-tutor scheme', *Educ. for Teaching*, **73**, 25–30.

BARNES, D. (1969) *Language, the Learner and the School* (revised edition, 1971), Penguin.

BARR, A. S. *et al.* (1961) 'Wisconsin studies of the measurement and prediction of teacher effectiveness: A summary of investigations', *J. Exper. Educ.*, **30**, 5–156.

BEARD, R. (1973) *Teaching and Learning in Higher Education*, 2nd edition, Penguin.

BELLACK, A. and DAVITZ, J. R. (1963) *The Language of the Classroom*, Teachers College Press, New York.

BELT, W. D. (1967) 'Microteaching: Observed and critiqued by a group of trainees vs. one instructor and one trainee', *AERA Conference Report*, New York.

BENNETT, D. J. and BENNETT, J. D. (1970) 'Making the scene', in COSIN, B. R. *et al.*, eds. (1971) *School and Society: A Sociological Reader*, Routledge & Kegan Paul.

BERLINER, D. C. (1969) *Microteaching and the Technical Skills Approach to Teacher Training*. Technical Report No. 8, Stanford University, California.

BERLYNE, D. E. (1962) *Conflict, Arousal and Curiosity*, McGraw-Hill.

BIDDLE, E. J. and ELLENA, W. J. (1964) *Contemporary Research on Teacher Effectiveness*, Holt, Rinehart & Winston.

BIRDWHISTELL, R. L. (1970) *Kinesics and Context: Essays in Body Motion Communication*, Allen Lane Press.

BISHOP, A. J. and WHITFIELD, R. C. (1972) *Situations in Teaching*, McGraw-Hill.

BLOOM, B. S., ed. (1956) *Taxonomy of Educational Objectives, Handbook I: The Cognitive Domain*, Longman (reprinted, 1965).

BLOOM, B. S. (1971) *Handbook of Summative and Evaluative Learning*, McGraw-Hill.

[156]   BONDI, J. C. (1970) 'Feedback from Interaction Analysis, some implications for the improvement of teaching', *J. Tchr. Educ.*, **21**, 189–96.

BORG, W. R., KALLENBACH, W., MORRIS, M. and FRIEBEL, A. (1969) 'Videotape feedback and microteaching in a teacher training model', *J. Exper. Educ.*, **37**, 9–16.

BORG, W. R., KELLEY, M. L., LANGER, P. and GALL, M. D. (1970) *The Minicourse: A Micro-teaching Approach to Teacher Education*, Collier Macmillan.

BRIMER, A. and COPE, E. (1972) *A Study of a School Based Practice*, University of Bristol School of Education.

BROWN, G. A. (1971) 'Microteaching: Innovation in teacher education', *Educ. for Teaching*, **86**, 11–15.

BROWN, G. A. (1971) 'Teacher Education at Ulster', *Times Educational Supplement*, 6 August, p. 17.

BROWN, G. A. (1973) 'The effects of training upon performance in teaching situations', Unpublished D.Phil. thesis, New University of Ulster, Coleraine.

BROWN, G. A. and GIBBS, I. (1974) 'Some students' reactions to microteaching', unpublished mimeo, New University of Ulster.

CHANAN, G. (1973) *Towards a Science of Teaching*, National Foundation for Educational Research.

CLEGG, A. (1965) 'Dangers ahead', *Education*, p. 240.

COHEN, L. (1965) 'An exploratory study of the teacher's role as perceived by head teachers, tutors and students in a training college', M.Ed. thesis, University of Liverpool.

COHEN, L. (1968) 'College and the training of teachers', *Educ. Res.*, **2**, 14–22.

COHEN, L. (1969) 'Students' perceptions of the school practice period', *Res. in Educ.*, **2**, 52–8.

COLLIER, K. G. (1959) 'The criteria of assessment of practical teaching', *Educ. for Teaching*, **48**, 36–40.

COLLINS, M. (1969) *Students into Teachers*, Routledge & Kegan Paul.

COOK, M. (1970), *Interpersonal Perception*, Penguin.

COOPER, J. M. and STROUD, E. (1967) 'Microteaching as a pre-internship training technique for the development of specific teaching skills', *AERA Conference Report*, New York.

COPE, E. (1970) 'Teacher training and school practice, *Educ. Res.*, **12**, 87–98.

COPE, E. (1971) *School Experience in Teacher Education*, University of Bristol School of Education.

CORSINI, R. J. and HOWARD, D. D. (1964) *Critical Incidents in Teaching*, Prentice-Hall.

COSIN, B. R. *et al.*, eds. (1971) *School and Society: A Sociological Reader*, Routledge & Kegan Paul in association with the Open University.

CRONBACH, L. S. (1966) 'The logic of experiments on discovery', in SHULMAN, L. S. and KEISLAR, E. R., eds. (1966), *Learning by Discovery*, Rand McNally.

DAVIES, D. and AMERSHEK, K. (1964) 'Student teaching', in EBEL, R. L. (1969) *Encyclopaedia of Educational Research*, 4th edition, Macmillan.

DAVIES, I. F. (1973) *The Management of Learning*, McGraw-Hill.

DAVIS, G. A. and HOUTMAN, S. E. (1968) *Thinking Creatively: A Guide to Training Imagination*, Wisconsin Research and Development Centre for Cognitive Learning.

DE BONO, D. (1970). *Lateral Thinking: A Text Book of Creativity*, Ward Lock.

DE BONO, E. *CoRT Thinking* (1973) Direct Education Services, Blandford Forum, Dorset.

DE CECCO, J. P., ed. (1967) *The Psychology of Learning and Instruction: Readings*, Holt, Rinehart and Winston.

DE CECCO, J. P. (1968) *The Psychology of Learning and Instruction*, Prentice-Hall.

DELANEY, D. J. and MOOR, J. C. (1967) 'Student expectations of the role of practicum super-visors', *Counsellor Education and Supervision*, **1**, 11–17.

DENT, H. C. (1971) 'An historical perspective', in HEWETT, S., ed. (1971) *The Training of Teachers: a Factual Survey*, University of London Press.

DUNKIN, M. and BIDDLE, B. (1973) *The Study of Teaching*, Holt, Rinehart & Winston.

EBEL, R. L. (1969) *Encyclopaedia of Educational Research*, 4th edition, Macmillan.

EVANS, D. R. (1970) 'Microteaching: An innovation in teacher education', *Education in Eastern Africa*, 1.

FANSLOW, W. W. (1965) 'Studies of attending behaviour', Doctoral thesis, Stanford University, California.

FLANDERS, N. A. (1968) 'Interaction analysis and service training', *J. Exper. Educ.*, 37, 126–33.

FLANDERS, N. A. (1970) *Analysing Teaching Behaviour*, Addison-Wesley.

FLANDERS, N. A. (1973) 'Basic teaching skills derived from a model of speaking and listening', *J. Tchr. Educ.*, 24, 24–37.

FLANDERS, N. A. and SIMON, A. (1969) 'Teacher effectiveness', in EBEL, R. L., ed. (1969) *Encyclopaedia of Educational Research*, Macmillan.

FORTUNE, J. C. et al. (1967) 'Stanford summer microteaching clinic 1965', *J. Tchr. Educ.*, 181, 389–93.

FOSTER, J. (1972) *Discovery Learning in the Primary School*, Routledge & Kegan Paul.

GAGE, N. L. (1963) *A Handbook of Research on Teaching*, Rand McNally.

GAGE, N. L. (1972) 'Explorations of teacher effectiveness in lecturing', in WESTBURY, I. and BELLACK, A. A., eds. (1972) *Research in Classroom Processes: Recent Developments and Next Steps*, Teachers College Press, New York.

GAGNE, R. M. (1965) 'Educational objectives and human performance', in KRUMBOLTZ, D., ed. (1965) *Learning and the Educational Process*, Rand McNally.

GAGNE, R. M. (1970) *The Conditions of Learning*, 2nd edition, Holt, Rinehart & Winston.

GALL, M. D. (1970) 'The use of questioning in teaching', *Rev. Educ. Res.*, 40, 707–21.

GALLOWAY, C. (1969), 'A model of teacher nonverbal communication', *Classroom Interaction Newsletter*, 4, 12–21.

GARNER, J. (1973) 'The nature of teaching and the effectiveness of teachers', in LOMAX, D. (1973), *The Education of Teachers in Britain*, J. Wiley & Sons.

GEORGIADES, N. (1972) 'A report on the L.U.S.T.I. project', Department of Occupational Psychology, Birkbeck College, University of London.

GETZELS, J. W. and JACKSON, P. W. (1963) 'The teacher's personality and characteristics', in GAGE, N. L., ed. (1963) *Handbook of Research on Teaching*, Rand McNally.

GLOVER, D. R. (1970) 'Experiences as a teacher tutor', *Educ. in Chem.*, 7, 185–6.

GOLDHAMMER, R. (1969) *Clinical Supervision: Special Methods for the Supervision of Teachers*, Rinehart & Winston.

GRAINGER, A. J. (1970) *The Bull Ring*, Pergamon.

GRIFFITHS, R. (1972) 'The role of the tutor in microteaching supervision', mimeo, Department of Education, University of Stirling.

GRIFFITHS, A. and MOORE, A. H. (1967) 'Schools and teaching practice', *Educ. for Teaching*, 74, 33–9.

GROBE, R. P. and PETTIBONE, T. J. (1973) 'Effects of instructional pace on student attentiveness', paper presented to Amer. Educ. Res. Assoc., New Orleans, February.

HARGREAVES, D.H. (1967) *Social Relations in a Secondary School*, Routledge & Kegan Paul.

HARGREAVES, D. H. (1972) *Interpersonal Relationships in Education*, Routledge & Kegan Paul.

HARVERSON, P. (1972) *Signs and Signals*, Penguin Primary Project, Penguin.

HELM, E. (1970) 'Teaching practice expenses in voluntary colleges', mimeo, St Martin's College of Education, Lancaster.

HEWETT, S., ed. (1971) *The Training of Teachers: A Factual Survey*, University of London Press.

HIRST, P. H. (1971) 'What is teaching?' *J. Curr. Studies*, 3, 5–18.

HORE, T. (1971) 'Assessment of teaching practice: An attractive hypothesis,' *Brit. J. Educ. Psychol.*, 41, 327.

[158] HOSPERS, J. (1967) *An Introduction to Philosophical Analysis*, 2nd edition, Routledge & Kegan Paul.

HUDSON, B. (1973) *Assessment Techniques : An Introduction*, Methuen.

HYMAN, C. T. ed. (1971) *Contemporary Thought on Teaching*, Prentice-Hall.

JAMES (Chairman) (1972) *Teacher Education and Training*, H.M.S.O.

JOHNSON, W. D. and KNAUPP, J. E. (1970) 'Trainee role expectations of the microteaching supervisor', *J. Tchr. Educ.*, 21, 396–401.

JOYCE, B. and WEIL, M. (1972) *Models of Teaching*, Prentice-Hall

KAHL, R., ed. (1963) *Studies in Explanation*, Prentice-Hall.

KALLENBACH, W. W. and GALL, M. D. (1969) 'Microteaching versus conventional methods in training elementary intern teachers', *J. Educ. Res.*, 63, 136–41.

KALTSOUNIS, T. and NELSON, J. L. (1968) 'The mythology of student teaching', *J. Tchr. Educ.*, 19, 277–82.

KLAUSMEIER, H. J. and RIPPLE, R. E. (1971) *Learning and Human Abilities*, 3rd edition, Harper & Row.

KORAN, J. J. (1969) 'Supervision: an attempt to modify behaviour', *Ed. Leadership*, 26, 759–67.

KOUNIN, J. S. (1967) 'An analysis of teachers' managerial techniques', *Psychology in the Schools*, 4, 221–7; reprinted in MORRISON, A. and MCINTYRE, D., eds. (1972) *The Social Psychology of Teaching*, Penguin.

KOUNIN, J. (1970) *Discipline and Group Management in Classrooms*, Holt, Rinehart & Winston.

KRUMBOLTZ, D., ed. (1965) *Learning and the Educational Process*, Rand McNally.

LACEY, D. (1970) *Hightown Grammar*, Manchester University Press.

LAWLESS, C. J. (1971) 'Microteaching without hardware: Developments at the University of Malawi', *Teacher Education in New Countries*, 12, 53–63.

LOMAX, D., ed. (1973) *The Education of Teachers in Britain*, J. Wiley & Sons.

LYNN, R. (1966) *Attention, Arousal and the Orientation Reaction*, Pergamon Press.

MACBETH, C. (1972) 'Students and probationers: An observational study', M.A. thesis, University of Dundee.

MACBETH, C. and MORRISON, A. (1972) 'Students and probationer teachers', *Durham Res. Rev.*, 6, 690–4.

MACLENNAN, D. (1974) 'The effects of teacher questions upon pupil attitudes and achievement: a study in the microteaching context', M.Sc. thesis, University of Stirling.

MACGRAW, F. M. (1965) 'The use of 35 mm time-lapse photography as a feedback and observation instrument in teacher education', Doctoral thesis, Stanford University, California.

MAGER, R. F. (1962) *Preparing Instructional Objectives*, Fearon Press, Palo Alto.

MAIER, N. R. F. (1958) *The Appraisal Interview*, J. Wiley & Sons.

MCALEESE, W. R. and UNWIN, D. (1971) 'Microteaching: A selective survey', *Programmed Learning and Educational Technology*, 8, 10–21.

MCCLEISH, J. (1968) *The Lecture Method*, Cambridge Monographs on Teaching Methods, No. 1, Cambridge Institute of Education.

MCINTYRE, D. and DUTHIE, J. (1971) 'Students' reactions to microteaching', mimeo, University of Stirling.

MCKEACHIE, W. J. (1963) 'Research on teaching at the college and university level', in GAGE, N. L., ed. (1963) *Handbook of Research on Teaching*, Rand McNally.

MCKNIGHT, P. (1971) 'Microteaching in teacher training: A review of research', *Res. in Educ.*, 6, 24–38; reprinted in MORRISON, A. and MCINTYRE, D., eds. (1972) *The Social Psychology of Teaching*, Penguin.

MCNAIR (Chairman) (1964), *Teachers and Youth Leaders*, H.M.S.O.

MEDLEY, D. M. and MITZEL, H. E. (1963) 'Measuring classroom behaviour by systematic [159] observation', in GAGE, N. L., ed. (1963), *Handbook of Research on Teaching*, Rand McNally.

MEIER, J. H. (1968) 'Rationale for and application of microteaching to improve teaching', *J. Tchr. Educ.*, 19, 145–57.

MEUX, M. and SMITH, B. O. (1964) 'Logical dimensions of teaching behaviour', in BIDDLE, E. J. and ELLENA, W. J. (1964) *Contemporary Research on Teacher Effectiveness*, Holt, Rinehart & Winston.

MORRISON, A. and MCINTYRE, D., eds. (1972) *Social Psychology of Teaching*, Penguin.

MORRISON, A. and MCINTYRE, D. (1973) *Teachers and Teaching*, 2nd edition, Penguin.

NASH, R. (1973) *Classroom Observed*, Routledge & Kegan Paul.

NICHOLS, R. G. (1957) *Are you listening?* McGraw-Hill.

PECK, R. F. and TUCKER, J. A. (1973) 'Research on teacher education', in TRAVERS, R. W. (1973) *Second Handbook of Research on Teaching*, Rand McNally.

PERRY, G. and PERRY, P. (1969) *Case Studies in Teaching*, Pitman.

PETERSON, A. D. C. (1966) *The Techniques of Teaching*, Vols I and II, Pergamon Press.

PINNEY, R. H. and DODGE, G. G. (1970) 'Variations of practice, location and supervision in an in-service programme' mimeo, Mid-West Regional Education Laboratory, Minnesota.

POPHAM, W. J. *et al.* (1969) *Instructional Objectives*, Rand McNally.

PRING, R. (1971) 'Bloom's Taxonomy: a philosophical critique', *Cambridge J. of Educ.*, 2, 83–91.

RIPPLE, R. E., ed. (1971) *Readings in Learning and Human Abilities*, 2nd edition, Harper & Row.

ROBERTSON, J. D. C. (1957) 'An analysis of the views of supervisors on the attributes of successful student teachers', *Brit. J. Educ. Psychol.*, 27, 115–26.

ROSENSHINE, B. (1968) 'Objectively measured behavioural predictors of effectiveness in explaining', *Technical Report No. 4*, Stanford Research and Development Centre in Teaching, California.

ROSENSHINE, B. (1970) 'Enthusiastic teaching: a research review', *School Rev.*, 78, 499–514; reprinted in MORRISON, A. and MCINTYRE, D., eds. (1972) *The Social Psychology of Teaching*, Penguin.

ROSENSHINE, B. (1971) *Teaching Behaviours and Student Achievement*, IEA Studies No. 1, National Foundation of Educational Research.

ROSENSHINE, B. and FURST, N. (1973) 'The use of direct observation to study teaching', in TRAVERS, R. W., ed. (1973) *Second Handbook of Research on Teaching*, Rand McNally.

RYAN, D. G. (1960) *The Characteristics of Teachers*. American Council of Education, Washington D.C.

RYLE, G. (1949) *The Concept of Mind*, Hutchinson.

SALOMON, G. and MCDONALD, F. J. (1970) 'Pretest and posttest reactions to self viewing one's teaching performance on videotape', *Brit. J. Educ. Psychol.*, 61, 280–6.

SANDERS, N. M. (1966) *Classroom Questions: What Kinds?* Harper & Row.

SHIPMAN, M. D. (1965) 'Personal and social influences on the work of a teacher training college,' Ph.D. thesis, University of London.

SHIPMAN, M. D. (1966) 'The assessment of teaching practice', *Educ. for Teaching*, No. 70, 28–31.

SHIPMAN, M. D. (1967) 'Theory and practice in the education of teachers', *Educ. Res.*, 9, 208–12.

SHULMAN, L. S. and KEISLAR, E. R., eds. (1966), *Learning by Discovery*, Rand McNally.

SIMON, A. and BOYER, G. E., eds. (1970; 2nd edition) *Mirrors for Behaviour: An Anthology of Classroom Observation Instruments*, Philadelphia Research for Better Schools.

SMITH, B. O. (1969a) 'A concept of teaching', *Teacher College Record*, 61, 229–41; reprinted in HYMAN, C. T. (1971) *Contemporary Thought on Teaching*, Prentice-Hall.

SMITH, B. O. (1969b) *Teachers for the Real World*, Amer. Assoc. of Colleges for Teacher Education.

SMITH, B. O. (1971) *Research in Teacher Education*, Prentice-Hall.

[160] SOCKETT, H. (1971) 'Bloom's Taxonomy: a philosophical critique (1)', *Cambridge J. of Educ.*, 1, 16–25.

SORENSON, G. (1967) 'What is learned in practice teaching?' *J. Tchr. Educ.*, 18, 173–8.

SPELMAN, B. (1974) 'Contrasting models of teacher effectiveness', D.Phil. thesis, New University of Ulster, Coleraine.

SPELMAN, B. J. and ST JOHN BROOKES, C. (1973) Microteaching and teacher education: A critical reappraisal', unpublished mimeo.

STANFORD (no author) (1968) 'Microteaching, a description', mimeo, Stanford University, California.

STENHOUSE, L. (1971) 'Some limitations of the use of objectives in curriculum research and planning', *Pedegogica Europaea*, 2, 73–83.

STEWIG, J. W. (1970) 'What should college supervisors do?' *J. Teacher Educ.*, 21, 251–7.

STONES, E. (1970) *Readings in Educational Psychology: Learning and Teaching*, Methuen.

STONES, E. and ANDERSON, D. (1972) *Educational Objectives and the Teaching of Educational Psychology*, Methuen.

STONES, E. and MORRIS, S. (1972a) 'The assessment of practical teaching', *Educ. Res.*, 14; and in 1972b.

STONES, E. and MORRIS, S. (1972b) *Teaching Practice, Problems and Perspectives*, Methuen.

STUART, S. (1969) *Say*, Nelson.

TAYLOR, J. K. and DALE, I. R. (1971) *A Survey of Teachers in their First Year of Service*, University of Bristol School of Education.

TAYLOR, W. (1973) 'Research and change in teacher education', paper read to the European Symposium on Research and Reform in Teacher Education, Bristol, April 1973.

THYNE, J. M. (1963) *The Psychology of Learning and Techniques of Teaching*, University of London Press.

TIBBLE, J. W., ed. (1971) *The Future of Teacher Education*, Routledge & Kegan Paul.

TIBBLE, J. W. (1971) 'The organization and supervision of school practice', in TIBBLE, J. W. (1971) *The Future of Teacher Education*, Routledge & Kegan Paul.

TRAVERS. R. W., ed. (1973) *The Second Handbook of Research on Teaching*, Rand McNally.

TRENT, J. W. and COHEN, A. M. (1973) 'Research on teaching in higher education', in TRAVERS, R. W., ed. (1973) *Second Handbook of Research on Teaching*. Rand McNally.

WAIMON, M. D. (1972) 'The effects of competency-based training on the performance of prospective teachers', *J. Tchr. Educ.*, 23, 68–79.

WARD, B. E. (1970) 'A survey of microteaching in secondary education programmes of all D.C.A.T.E. accredited colleges and universities', *Memorandum No. 70*, Stanford Centre for Research and Development in Teaching, California.

WESTBURY, I. and BELLACK, A. A. (1972) *Research in Classroom Processes: Recent Developments and Next Steps*, Teachers' College Press, New York.

WITTROCK, M. C. (1962) 'Set applied to teaching', *J. Educ. Psychol.*, 53, 175–80.

WITTROCK, M. C. (1966) 'The learning by discovery hypothesis', in SHULMAN, L. S. and KEISLAR, E. R., eds. (1966) *Learning by Discovery*, Rand McNally.

WORTHEN, B. R. (1968) 'A study of discovery of exposition presentation: Implications for teaching', *J. Tchr. Educ.*, 19, 223–42.

WRAGG, E. C. (1972) 'An analysis of the verbal classroom interaction between graduate student teachers and pupils', Ph.D. thesis, University of Exeter.

WRAGG, E. C. 1973) 'A study of student teachers in the classroom', in CHANNAN, G., ed. (1973) *Towards a Science of Teaching*, National Foundation of Educational Research.

WRAGG, E. C. (1975) *Teaching Teaching*, David & Charles.

WRIGHT, C. J. and NUTHALL, G. (1970) 'The relationships between teacher behaviours and pupil achievement in three experimental elementary science lessons', *Amer. Educ. Res. J.*,

7, 477–91. Reprinted in MORRISON, and MCINTYRE (1973) *Teachers and Teaching*, 2nd ed. Penguin.

YOUNG, D. B. (1970) 'Preliminary report on the effectiveness of colleague supervision on the acquisition of selected teaching behaviours in a microteaching series', paper presented at the annual conference of the Amer. Educ. Res. Assoc.

Index